Upper Columbia Basin Network Osprey Monitoring Protocol

Narrative Version 1.0

Natural Resource Report NPS/UCBN/NRR—2010/269

Lisa K. Garrett
National Park Service, Upper Columbia Basin Network
105 East 2nd St. Suite #5
Moscow, ID 83843

Thomas J. Rodhouse
National Park Service, Upper Columbia Basin Network
20310 Empire Ave. Suite A100
Bend, OR 97701

Gordon H. Dicus
National Park Service, Upper Columbia Basin Network
105 East 2nd St. Suite #6
Moscow, ID 83843

Paulina F. Tobar-Starkey
National Park Service, Upper Columbia Basin Network
105 East 2nd St. Suite #7
Moscow, ID 83843

December 2010

U.S. Department of the Interior
National Park Service
Natural Resource Program Center
Fort Collins, Colorado

The National Park Service, Natural Resource Program Center publishes a range of reports that address natural resource topics of interest and applicability to a broad audience in the National Park Service and others in natural resource management, including scientists, conservation and environmental constituencies, and the public.

The Natural Resource Report Series is used to disseminate high-priority, current natural resource management information with managerial application. The series targets a general, diverse audience, and may contain NPS policy considerations or address sensitive issues of management applicability.

All manuscripts in the series receive the appropriate level of peer review to ensure that the information is scientifically credible, technically accurate, appropriately written for the intended audience, and designed and published in a professional manner. This report received formal, high-level peer review based on the importance of its content, or its potentially controversial or precedent-setting nature. Peer review was conducted by highly qualified individuals with subject area technical expertise and was overseen by a peer review manager.

Views, statements, findings, conclusions, recommendations, and data in this report do not necessarily reflect views and policies of the National Park Service, U.S. Department of the Interior. Mention of trade names or commercial products does not constitute endorsement or recommendation for use by the U.S. Government.

This report is available from the Upper Columbia Basin Network website (http://www.nature.nps.gov/im/units/UCBN) and the Natural Resource Publications Management website (http://www.nature.nps.gov/publications/NRPM).

NPS 963/106166, December 2010

Change History

Original Version #	Date of Revision	Revised By	Changes	Justification	New Version #

1. Version numbers increase incrementally by tenths (e.g., version 1.1, version 1.2, ...etc) for minor changes. Major revisions should be designated with the next whole number (e.g., version 2.0, 3.0, 4.0 ...). Record the previous version number, date of revision, author of the revision, identify paragraphs and pages where changes are made, and the reason for making the changes along with the new version number.

2. Notify the UCBN Data Manager of any changes to the Protocol Narrative or SOPs so that the new version number can be incorporated in the Metadata of the project database.

3. Post new versions on the internet and forward copies to all individuals with a previous version of the Protocol Narrative or SOPs. A list will be maintained in an appendix at the end of this document.

Contents

Contents

Contents

Figures

Tables

Appendixes

Executive Summary

The mission of the National Park Service is "to conserve unimpaired the natural and cultural resources and values of the national park system for the enjoyment of this and future generations" (NPS 1999). To uphold this goal, the Director of the NPS approved the Natural Resource Challenge to encourage national parks to focus on the preservation of the nation's natural heritage through science, natural resource inventories, and expanded resource monitoring (NPS 1999). Through the Challenge, 270 parks in the national park system were organized into 32 inventory and monitoring networks.

The Upper Columbia Basin Network (UCBN) has identified 14 priority park vital signs, indicators of ecosystem health, which represent a broad suite of ecological phenomena operating across multiple temporal and spatial scales. Our intent has been to develop a balanced and integrated "package" of vital signs that meets the needs of current park management, but will also be able to accommodate unanticipated environmental conditions in the future. Osprey (*Pandion haliaetus*) abundance is a particularly high priority vital sign for Lake Roosevelt National Recreation Area (LARO). Osprey monitoring is a critical element in the suite of information needed by LARO managers to adequately understand and manage park ecological condition. Indicator species help researchers and resource managers by providing information on the overall condition of an ecosystem. For several reasons raptors can be extremely useful indicators of environmental change. Raptors occupy most ecosystems, cover large home ranges, are often migratory, top predators in complex food webs, and are sensitive to environmental contaminants and other human disturbances (Bildstein 2001). Ospreys are an excellent example of an indicator species, and have been proposed as a worldwide sentinel species for monitoring environmental contaminants in rivers, lakes, reservoirs, and estuaries (Grove et al. 2009).

This protocol details the why, where, how, and when of the UCBN's osprey monitoring program. As recommended by Oakley et al. (2003), it consists of a protocol narrative and a set of standard operating procedures (SOPs), which detail the steps required to collect, manage, and disseminate the data representing the status and trend of osprey populations at LARO. The protocol is a "living" document in the sense that it is continually updated as new information acquired through monitoring and evaluation leads to refinement of program objectives and methodologies. Changes to the protocol are carefully documented in a revision history log. The intent of the protocol is to ensure that a seamless and scientifically credible story about osprey populations and their supporting habitat and environmental conditions can be told to park visitors and park managers alike. The story is already beginning to unfold. Two years of pilot data have been collected and park rangers have begun incorporating results from the osprey monitoring into their interpretive programs. The next few years of monitoring results are eagerly awaited, as outstanding questions related to status in osprey nest occupancy and productivity are answered and the current location of nest sites can finally be described. From there, the focus will shift toward trend analysis, in which biologically meaningful declines or increases will be detected.

Acknowledgments

Funding for this project was provided through the National Park Service Natural Resource Challenge and the Servicewide Inventory and Monitoring Program. We thank the resource management staff at Lake Roosevelt National Recreation Area who provided assistance with pilot data collection efforts, logistical support with boats and housing, and thorough and constructive comments on earlier versions of this protocol. Kathi Irvine provided helpful advice regarding the treatment of survey and analysis decisions.

Background and Objectives

Rationale for Monitoring Osprey Populations at Lake Roosevelt National Recreation Area

Indicator species help researchers and resource managers by providing information on the overall condition of an ecosystem. For several reasons raptors can be extremely useful indicators of environmental change. Raptors occupy most ecosystems, cover large home ranges, are often migratory, top predators in complex food webs, and are sensitive to environmental contaminants and other human disturbances (Bildstein 2001). The osprey is an excellent example of one of these indicator species.

Many characteristics of osprey make them ideal biological indicators. Ospreys roost and nest on poles or snags and they build massive and conspicuous stick nests typically adjacent to fish-bearing waters (Henny et al. 1978), making them ideal candidates for assessing changes in nest occupancy and productivity. Ospreys feed almost exclusively on live fish captured at or near the water's surface (Bent 1937) and individual pairs show variation in the ability to tolerate human activity (Van Daele and Van Daele 1982). Ospreys are long-lived, mate for life, and typically return to the same nest each year (US Geological Survey 2003). One of the largest birds in North America, osprey were historically reported as numerous and widespread. Through the mid-1970's, osprey populations drastically declined as a result of pesticide use. Most populations, following the ban of several pesticides, have since recovered and, to some extent, adapted to human-dominated landscapes, nesting on power poles, cellular towers, and channel markers when suitable natural nest sites are scarce (Ewins 1997, US Geological Survey 2003). Ospreys are currently found throughout the Columbia River system, including along Lake Roosevelt, where this protocol is focused.

North American osprey populations began to drastically decline in the early 1950s and declines continued through the early 1970s (Reese 1972, Poole 1989). Environmental pollutants such as Dieldrin, Dichlorodiphenyldichloroethylene (DDE), and Polychlorinated biphenyls (PCBs), have been listed as the primary cause of declines. These pollutants bioaccumulate in the aquatic flora and fauna and, since fish constitute 99% of an osprey's diet, pollutants accumulate rapidly in osprey tissue. At high levels, these contaminants cause eggshell thinning and decreased egg viability (Ames 1966, Wiemeyer et al. 1978, Steidl et al. 1991). With restrictions and bans on many of these pollutants in the 1980s, osprey numbers have rebounded and are flourishing in many areas (Titus and Fuller 1990). However, the presence of contaminants still remains a concern in many areas, including in Lake Roosevelt National Recreation Area (LARO). Several recent osprey-contaminant studies in the region have detailed the spatial extent and level of contamination (Elliott et al. 1998, 2000, 2001, Henny et al. 2003, 2004, Henny et al. 2008, Henny et al. 2009a). Flame retardants (polybrominated diphenyl ethers), are emerging contaminants and have shown increasing concentrations in osprey eggs in recent years, with possible effects on reproductive success (Henny et al, 2009b).

LARO was established as a unit of the national park system in 1946 by the Secretary of the Interior. With the Secretary's approval, an agreement between the Bureau of Reclamation, the Bureau of Indian Affairs, and the NPS designated the NPS as the manager for the Coulee Dam National Recreation Area. The area included Franklin D. Roosevelt Lake, the reservoir formed behind Grand Coulee Dam, and the "freeboard" lands that were purchased at and above 1,310 foot elevation. Through over 50 years of changes, including a name change to Lake Roosevelt National Recreation Area in 1997, the NPS now manages approximately 47,438 acres of the 81,389 acres of total water surface and associated shoreline, and 12,936 acres of the 19,196 acres of total freeboard land. Also, in 1990, two adjacent Indian Tribes were included in the Lake Roosevelt Cooperative Management Agreement. The Colville Confederated Tribe and the Spokane Tribe of Indians manage the remaining water surface and freeboard land.

The LARO General Management Plan (NPS 2000) defines the 3 major purposes for the recreation area:
  • Provide opportunities for diverse, safe, quality, outdoor recreation experiences for the public.
  • Preserve, conserve, and protect the integrity of natural, cultural, and scenic resources.
  • Provide opportunities to enhance public appreciation and understanding about the area's significant resources.

LARO offers a variety of recreation opportunities in a diverse natural setting on a 154- mile-long lake bordered by 312 miles of publicly owned shoreline. Visitation at the park has fluctuated between a high of 1,784,420 (1990) to a low of 1,081,112 (1996) and has averaged 1,374,797 between 1990 and 2004. LARO has 5 marinas, 3 with campgrounds, and numerous overnight and day-use campgrounds and points of access around the lake. The recreation area includes the lower reaches of many rivers and streams including the Spokane and Kettle Rivers.

The osprey is a common breeding resident in LARO and is at risk of environmental contamination. Contaminants found in the sediments of the Upper Columbia River consist of heavy metals such as antimony, arsenic, cadmium, copper, lead, mercury, and zinc, and organic contaminants such as polychlorinated dibenzo-p-dioxins (dioxins), polychlorinated dibenzofurans (furans), and PCBs (Environmental Protection Agency 2006). Known and potential sources of contaminants in LARO include mining and milling operations, smelting operations, pulp and paper production, sewage treatment plants, and other industrial activities (Environmental Protection Agency 2006). One of the largest sources of contamination in LARO is the TechCominco Smelter, located along the Columbia River approximately 16 km (10 mi) north of the US border. This smelter has been discharging pollutants for over 100 years, making it the single largest source of heavy metal contaminants in the Upper Columbia River (Environmental Protection Agency 2006).

In the spring of 2006, the U.S. Environmental Protection Agency (EPA) reached an agreement with Teck Cominco (now called Teck) to conduct a Remedial Investigation and Feasibility Study (RI/FS) of the Upper Columbia River, which includes Lake Roosevelt. Typically, an RI/FS is conducted after EPA designates an area a Superfund site. Such a designation, and the actions that follow, are guided by the Comprehensive Environmental Response, Compensation and Liability Act (CERCLA). Created in 1980, this federal law enables EPA to clean up hazardous waste sites and compel responsible parties to conduct or fund EPA directed cleanups.

Lake Roosevelt, however, was not declared a Superfund site. Instead, the 2006 agreement reached with Teck allows EPA to carry out an RI/FS and other CERCLA processes without a Superfund designation being imposed.

Given the extent of contamination in Lake Roosevelt, avian piscivores such as osprey are particularly at risk of bioaccumulation. As a top predator, osprey is one of the most vulnerable members of the aquatic ecosystem with regard to contamination effects. Studies have shown that many contaminants of concern biomagnify from fish to osprey eggs, sometimes by factors of 10-200 (Henny et al. 2003).

Increased human recreational activity is an additional stressor on osprey populations in LARO. While reservoirs and man-made nesting structures such as telephone poles and artificial platforms benefit osprey, high levels of human activity in the vicinity of occupied nests may be adversely affecting successful reproduction (D'Eon and Watt 1994). The effect of human disturbance on osprey is dependent on several factors including the timing, frequency, and intensity of disturbance and the degree of osprey habituation. Recreational activity at LARO has been steadily increasing over time, and in 2005, LARO attracted over 1 million visitors. Most of these are summertime watercraft users, and because osprey typically nests on or near the lakeshore and forage exclusively over open water, an inherent conflict exists.

In addition to bioaccumulation and human disturbance, Figure 1 illustrates the relationships among other external and internal sources of stress to osprey populations in the upper Columbia Basin. Competition for food with other piscivore species (e.g., double-crested cormorant (*Phalacrocorax auritus)*, Northern river otter (*Lontra canadensis*) and nest predation from raccoons (*Procyon lotor)* and great-horned owls (*Bubo virginianus*) can influence osprey population dynamics (Ewins 1997). While osprey are fairly well adapted to anthropogenic disturbances (Henny and Kaiser 1996, US Geological Survey 2003), changes in land cover/land use, climate, and/or invasive species that result in loss of nesting habitat may impact osprey populations at LARO. In particular, the absence of large snags in the intensively managed forests surrounding the northern portion of the Lake may result in fewer available nests and limit osprey populations. Severe wind storms and unusually cold, wet springs during the nesting season may result in the nests, with contents, being blown from the more exposed snags or result in nesting mortality due to exposure (Johnson et al. 2008). These factors, in addition to manipulation of water levels, hydroperiod, and flushing rate, influence the integrity of the lake itself (see Figure 1) and can impact bird communities indirectly through effects on fish and ability of osprey to capture fish in deep water (osprey capture fish near the surface).

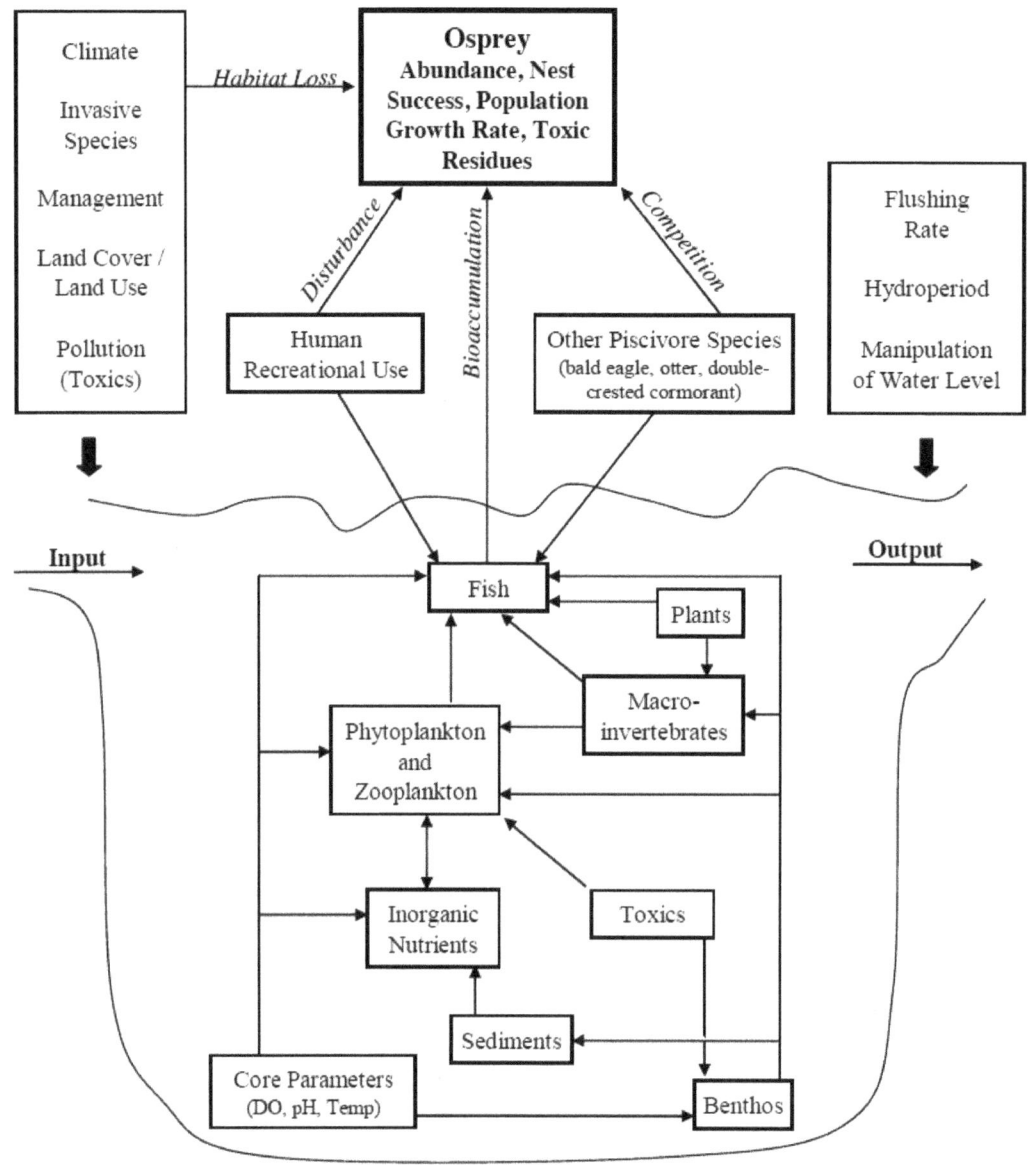

Figure 1. Conceptual model developed to illustrate the external and internal sources of stress on osprey populations at Lake Roosevelt National Recreation Area (lentic system).

Ospreys are known to consume a variety of fish species so species of fish is not as important as size of prey species (Vana-Miller 1987). Although ospreys usually select benthic-feeding fish because they are easier to capture, any medium-sized (15-35 cm) fish feeding in shallow water can be part of the diet. The diet in ospreys can change among and within years due to prey availability but the size of the prey appears consistently in the same size range.

Reservoirs, such as Lake Roosevelt, frequently contain fisheries composed primarily of non-native fishes. The illegal or intentional introduction of non-native game and forage fishes has been widespread (Rahel 2002). Important introduced fish species in the region include walleye, centrarchid sunfishes, brook and brown trout, carp, tench, large- and smallmouth bass, yellow perch, and black crappie. As part of mitigation offset for anadromous salmonid returns blocked by hydropower dams (Scholz et al. 1985), large numbers of kokanee (resident, non-anadromous sockeye salmon) and rainbow trout continue to be released annually to Lake Roosevelt. These fisheries have failed to meet management goals in terms of production, perhaps due to predation (including walleye; Baldwin et al. 2003), downstream entrainment in Grand Coulee Dam, and hatchery practices (McLellan et al. 2004). Despite this altered fish community, Lake Roosevelt appears to harbor a stable or growing population of burbot, a native species thought to be in decline regionally (Bonar et al. 2000).

Ospreys are currently listed as a "monitor" species in Washington State with status intended for the protection of nesting locations (WDFW 2009a, WDFW 2009b). The osprey is no longer federally listed as threatened under the ESA, although the Gifford Pinchot National Forest Land and Resource Management Plan (LRMP), as amended by the 1995 Northwest Forest Plan, does reference the osprey and prescribe a protective buffer of approximately 660 feet around each identified nest site (Energy Northwest 2005). The Gifford National Forest is located in the southern Cascade Mountains of Washington State.

Well articulated desired future condition statements have not yet been developed for the osprey populations at LARO. However, the mission statements for the NPS as a whole and for LARO clearly state the intent "to conserve unimpaired the natural and cultural resources and values of the national park system for the enjoyment of this and future generations" (NPS 1999). We assume that desired future conditions for LARO will include a robust population of osprey that, when nesting, provides visitors a visual experience as they boat or recreate at the beaches in the recreation area. We also assume that current osprey nesting densities are minimally acceptable, and that an increase in osprey density is a reasonable goal for park management. Some form of artificial nesting structures constructed along the shoreline of LARO has been suggested to stimulate nesting and could be used as a tool to increase the population density of piscivorous birds. Also, retention and recruitment of large snags along the lake shore, where hazards can be mitigated, may also prove beneficial for the LARO osprey population. However, before any effort to increase osprey nesting populations is attempted park managers should determine if osprey populations along the shores of LARO have been exposed to contaminants such as would be introduced by pesticide or heavy metal contamination in their prey base. Efforts to increase osprey productivity or nesting success should be predicated on reasoning that the existing population is healthy and is only lacking suitable nesting structures in order to nest and fledge additional young.

Monitoring of osprey is a critical element in the suite of information needed by LARO managers to adequately understand and manage park ecological condition. Though there have been several studies over recent years examining the presence of contaminants within LARO, little information is available regarding osprey in the area and few studies (if any) have researched the potential impacts of these contaminants on osprey and other avian wildlife (Henny 2005). The Upper Columbia Basin Network (UCBN) Inventory and Monitoring (I & M) Program seeks to support LARO staff by developing a simple and effective long-term monitoring protocol that will provide timely information on osprey nesting distribution, abundance, and productivity. We will assist LARO in the identification of desired target values for occupancy and productivity, and conservative thresholds that, if crossed, might trigger management action. Because of the complexity of land ownership and management responsibilities in the Lake Roosevelt area, NPS management options are limited. However, osprey declines exceeding established thresholds may be used to garner support among other area stakeholders to support additional research or alternative management strategies.

Objectives

The overarching goal of the UCBN osprey vital signs monitoring program is to inform park resource managers about the status and trend of osprey populations at LARO. The primary objective of current osprey population management at LARO is to prevent a decline in current density levels. Knowledge of nest site characteristics and determining patterns in nesting area occupancy and reproductive success is important in the conservation and preservation of osprey populations.

Given the lack of available ecological data on osprey nesting ecology in LARO, the following fundamental questions continue to drive much of the UCBN's inquiry into osprey population ecology:

- What is the number of nests occupied in LARO? What is the trend in nest occupancy?
- What is the trend in productivity as measured by the number of young produced per occupied nest in LARO?
- What are the habitat characteristics of osprey nest sites at LARO?
- What volunteer programs can park managers implement to engage park staff and visitors in a greater appreciation for natural resources within LARO?

In light of these questions and the broader goals outlined above, this protocol will address the following specific measurable monitoring objectives:

1) Determine status and trend in the number of occupied osprey nests within 1500 m of Lake Roosevelt. *Justification: Currently little information is available concerning osprey nesting activity in LARO. Osprey nests are relatively easy to locate and observe. Locating nests will provide information regarding nest structure and it will also help to identify critical areas for increased protection.*

2) Determine status and trend in productivity (expressed as the number of young per occupied nest) for monitored osprey nests at LARO. *Justification: Productivity is essential to maintaining a healthy population. Contaminants and human disturbance at LARO may be affecting osprey*

productivity. Knowing the level of productivity of this area will help managers better understand population condition and proceed to address issues of management concern.

3) Determine status and trend in osprey nest site characteristics including nest tree metrics and habitat characteristics to evaluate changes in nesting habitat association for monitored osprey nests at LARO. ***Justification:*** *Currently little information is available concerning habitat characteristics of osprey nest sites in LARO. Collecting data on nest site characteristics will provide information regarding nest trees and use of artificial nest structures at LARO.*

4) Increase appreciation and understanding of osprey breeding biology and nest site requirements at LARO through the recruitment of park staff, local birdwatchers, and school groups in collecting and reporting osprey nest site data. ***Justification:*** *Currently one of the long-term goals of the resource staff is to increase public appreciation and understanding for the natural resources at LARO. The challenge is to help visitors understand that the national recreation area offers more than just fishing and boating opportunities. With a well-planned and well-delivered volunteer monitoring program for observation of osprey nests, visitors can collect and report data on osprey nest sites that will provide a means to increase public understanding and appreciation of osprey breeding biology.*

Survey Design

Survey Design Rationale

The objectives and survey design were developed, revised, and refined through a process that involved site reconnaissance, pilot data collection and analysis, and thoughtful consideration of park and network information requirements. The development team consisted of this document's authors, and the LARO resource manager.

This protocol is designed to support annual surveys of all occupied and accessible osprey nest locations within 1500 m of the Lake Roosevelt shoreline, and therefore does not involve a sampling design per se. We chose to survey the entire population of occupied and accessible nests rather than draw a random sample of nests. The decision to census is based on the fact that the total number of occupied and accessible nest sites is less than 30 nests making a census feasible. Also, the resource manager indicated the need to know about the productivity at particular nests in management areas of interest, and it was impossible to predict which nests would be involved in projects in any given year. Consequently, we wanted to know nest condition and nesting status at as many sites as possible, annually. If the nesting population increases considerably, we will add additional crews or volunteers in order to complete surveys and annual reports on time. Survey schedules, use of volunteers and biologists from other organizations, areas covered by aerial and ground surveys, record keeping systems, ways of collecting reports from others, and annual data summary methods will be adapted to fulfill our objectives and take advantage of available technologies.

A decision to monitor all occupied and accessible nest sites followed naturally from a consideration of the direct one-to-one connection between the number of occupied nest sites and osprey productivity. The rate of recruitment of osprey into the established population at LARO is not known at this early stage in the monitoring effort, however, a study in the West Kootenay region of British Columbia indicated the average number of young per occupied nest was 1.07 (Arndt 2007). Henny and Wight (1969) calculated that an annual productivity of 0.95 – 1.30 young was necessary in order to maintain a stable population.

Pilot Datasets

Records obtained from the Washington Department of Fish and Wildlife (WDFW) indicate that osprey nest sites along LARO were monitored on an intermittent and opportunistic basis by state biologists from 1971-2000. A standard monitoring protocol was not followed but the location of nest sites was recorded along with the type of nest structure. The most nests located within any one year were 12 with several years having data recorded for only 1 nest location.

GPS coordinates obtained from WDFW inventory data were used in an initial aerial survey flown in a fixed wing Cessna 206 to locate occupied nests in 2007. The primary objectives of this survey were to fly the entire length of the reservoir to determine the feasibility of completing a fixed wing survey in one day, and also to determine if the number of nest sites with known GPS coordinates from the WDFW surveys could be located from the air. Coordinates from the WDFW 1971-2000 inventories were uploaded to Garmin 76CSX GPS units. These previously inventoried nest locations were circled by the aircraft and observers on board attempted to assess whether the nest was occupied. Six nests were located using the historical data, and of these 6 nests, only 3 appeared to be occupied. The aerial survey was conducted on August 9, 2007 which is later than ideal to determine nest activity. Martell et al. (2001) found that the range of departure dates for osprey from the Willamette Valley, Oregon to their wintering grounds along the west coast of Mexico was from August 28-September 24. By early August most osprey young will have already fledged and nest activity will be decreasing (Table 1). The nesting chronology for LARO may be a little later (10-14 days) than in the Williamette Valley shown in Table 1, because it is located at a more northern latitude and elevation.

In 2008, LARO personnel conducted foot and boat surveys to locate occupied nests. This survey was conducted by Student Conservation Association (SCA) interns and was scheduled opportunistically by the LARO resource manager to gain information on osprey nesting activity to inform protocol development. Surveys were conducted periodically from July 24–August 1, 2008. Ten occupied osprey nests were observed. GPS coordinates were obtained for all occupied nests and the type of nest structure was recorded. Photographs were also taken of nest structures during this 2008 pilot data collection effort.

In 2009, LARO personnel conducted foot and boat surveys, using 2008 known nest site data, to locate occupied nests. Once again, this survey was scheduled opportunistically and SCA interns conducted the surveys from July 6-14, 2009. Nine of 26 nests surveyed were occupied and 4 nests contained at least 1 fledgling. The occupied nests were concentrated in the south end of Lake Roosevelt, between Keller Ferry and Porcupine Bay on the Spokane River.

Target Population

The target population for estimating the status and trend of osprey populations at LARO includes all occupied nests (known nests from previous years plus newly located nests during the mid-May survey for occupancy) identified and mapped within 1500 m of the shoreline of LARO. This population will include most, if not all, of the nesting ospreys that use Lake Roosevelt for their primary source of food. A study conducted in Yellowstone National Park (Swenson 1981) found that the distance to water of osprey nests varied from 2 to 1,430m with the mean at 121m. Two aerial surveys will be conducted once every 3 years that will aid in gaining information on new nest sites and any nest sites where access may be an issue. Ground-based surveys will be conducted during years when the aerial surveys are not scheduled to provide supplemental information to the aerial monitoring program.

Survey Frequency and Timing

Triennial helicopter surveys will be scheduled to document new nest sites and record productivity of nesting ospreys (Table 1). On years when aerial surveys are not scheduled supplemental information will be collected by foot, car, and boat to find laying pairs of osprey and to count fledglings.

Table 1. Osprey survey method schedule from 2011 through 2018.

YEAR	2011	2012	2013	2014	2015	2016	2017	2018
Survey Method	Helicopter	Ground	Ground	Helicopter	Ground	Ground	Helicopter	Ground

Two visits to nest sites during the breeding season are required in order to determine reproductive success of a nesting osprey pair (Postupalsky 1974). The first visit, made during early incubation, will be to determine if the site is occupied. Melquist (1974) determined that egg-laying and incubation commences during the month of May and that clutches are usually complete by the middle of May in populations of osprey in northern Idaho and northeastern Washington. This first survey, scheduled annually in mid-May, is the "activity" survey and is used to establish the number of occupied osprey nests in the target population. All known nest sites from the target population will be checked during this mid-May annual survey to determine occupancy. We will also search for new nests during this annual "activity" survey. When the initial survey is conducted during the 38-day incubation period, there should be an adult incubating on the nest essentially 100% of the time. If you are too early or too late, then it becomes difficult to determine what is going on at each nest. Timing of the first and second surveys is critical.

A second visit, called the "productivity survey," will be made just prior to the time that young fledge, and is to determine the outcome of nesting or the number of young fledged. Young will be counted when they are large enough to be seen from a distance, but not so late in the season that they have left the nest. The best time is just prior to the earliest known fledging dates for the particular region. The most relevant dates that we have established are July 8-15th, which is reported for an osprey population in Oregon (US Geological Survey 2003) shown in Table 2. If feathered nestlings are observed, and a determination can be made as to how many there are, or if a determination can be made that the nesting attempt failed, no further visits are required. If the number of nestlings is uncertain, downy nestlings are observed, or outcome is uncertain, additional visits are required. The goal is to determine the number of feathered nestlings. Late in the season if a nest fails, sometimes pairs will build a new nest (often called a frustration nest) near their old nest. These nests should not be counted as occupied nests. Biologists or volunteers will return weekly until outcome of nesting is determined and the number of feathered nestlings is counted. Standard operating procedures (SOPs) for checking nests from a helicopter are included in SOP #9 and from land or water are included in SOP #4.

Once every 3 years, a helicopter survey (SOP # 9) will replace the annual ground-based "activity" and "productivity" surveys. The methods for using helicopters in conducting nesting surveys of osprey populations is well-established (Carrier and Melquist 1976) and will enable data collection to occur over a large study area in a short period of time. It is probable that conducting surveys from the air may increase the likelihood of detecting a higher number of occupied nest sites.

One of the primary objectives of this protocol is to increase appreciation and understanding of osprey breeding biology and nest site requirements at LARO through the recruitment of park staff, local birdwatchers, and school groups in collecting and reporting osprey nest site data. Keeping this objective in mind, helicopter surveys conducted once every 3 years, will provide a means of possibly obtaining a larger sample size of occupied nests that in subsequent years can be visited by volunteers.

Table 2. Osprey Nesting Chronology, Willamette Valley, Oregon (US Geological Survey 2003).

Osprey Nesting Chronology, Williamette Valley, Oregon	
Arrival at nest sites	March 20 – April 15
Clutch completion	April 13 – May 20
Hatching	May 21 – June 27
First flight of young	July 15 – August 21
Departure to wintering grounds	August 20 – September 25

Response Design

Our terminology and data summary methods are based on Postupalsky (1974, 1983) and Steenhof and Newton (2007) who both recommended standard terminology for describing occupied nests and for calculating productivity.

Occupied Nests

Postupalsky (1974) noted that the term "occupied" has been applied in different ways by different authors, and concluded that only nests with evidence of actual pairs be counted as occupied. Following Postupalsky (1974), the following definition is used to determine if a nest is occupied (Table 2).

Table 3. Description of an occupied nest (Postupalsky 1974).

An occupied nest is defined as any nest at which one of the following activity patterns is observed during a given breeding season:
a) Young were raised;
b) Eggs were laid;
c) Two adults are present on or near the nest, regardless of whether or not it had been repaired during the season under consideration, provided there is no reason to suspect that this pair had already been counted elsewhere;
d) One adult is observed sitting low in the nest, presumably incubating;
e) One adult and one bird in immature plumage at or near a nest, if mating behavior (display flights, nest repair, coition) was observed.
f) A recently repaired nest with fresh sticks (clean breaks), or fresh boughs on top, and/or droppings and/or molten feathers on its rim or underneath. Such evidence is acceptable especially late in the season in cases where no earlier check was made.

All of the above observations indicate the known or inferred presence of 1 pair of birds associated with a nest. One adult near an empty, unrepaired nest or two adults seen together during the breeding season with no known nest is not sufficient evidence for an occupied nest. (Postupalsky 1974).

Productivity

Productivity is the number of young that reach the minimum acceptable age for assessing success and is usually reported as the number of young produced per occupied nest in a particular year (Postupalsky 1983). Postupalsky (1983) recommended counting young when adults are no longer brooding consistently, and young are large and dark (fully feathered). Our goal is to determine the number of feathered nestlings, but occasionally downy nestlings may be present during the second visit to a site. When this happens, an additional visit will be made to the nest site several days later to determine if the chicks are fully feathered or until they fly (fledge). Productivity is calculated as the number of young produced divided by the total number of occupied nests (young/occupied nest).

Nest Site Characteristics

Information collected on nest tree site characteristics will assist park managers in determining the location and type of structure that osprey are using for their nests along the shoreline of LARO. Nest site covariates that are recorded at occupied nest sites include: nest height (m), tree height (m), tree diameter at breast height (cm), distance to water (m), species of tree, and height and diameter of the 4 nearest trees that reach at least the lower canopy height of the nest tree (Edwards and Collopy 1988). Additional information on methods for collection of nest site characteristics is described in SOP #4.

Change Detection

Given the history of osprey population declines world-wide in response to environmental contamination, and the current level of contamination and human disturbance present in Lake Roosevelt, we have focused our analytical attention on detecting declines rather than increases, although our protocol will support change detection in both directions. Power to detect change is a function of sample size (occupied nests), magnitude of the minimum detectable change, and acceptable error (Type I and Type II error; Gerodette 1987). We have no ability to adjust the sample size, and have chosen to accept a higher Type I (false-change) error in order to minimize the Type II (β, or missed-change) error, reducing the "conservationist's risk" (Irwin 2006; Morrison 2007). Because we are observing most and potentially all members of the target population (mapped and accessible established nests), there will be little or no uncertainty in status estimates of occupancy or productivity, and therefore no requirement for power analysis or sample size calculations for status. Change detection will be restricted to the absolute increase or decrease in the number of occupied nests observed during the incubation period, and in the ratio of the total number of fledglings produced per year to the total number of occupied nests within the target population. We have taken a simulation approach to estimating power to detect declines for fixed sample sizes (occupied nests), and with Type I error (α or false-change error) fixed at 20%. In our case, year (time) is the variable that influences power, rather than sample size (number of nests) within years. Based on our simulations, power (1-β) to detect 50% declines in the number of occupied nests over 20 years with non-parametric Mann-Kendall tests will be approximately 95%.

Management Response Trigger

Following each annual osprey nesting cycle the UCBN and LARO staff together will consider the direction and magnitude of change, and resulting management response required for any annual change in occupied osprey nests. If the number of young osprey per occupied nest is consistently below the 0.95 minimum (the recognized production standard for maintaining a stable population of ospreys) for several years, additional investigations into contaminants, food habits studies, etc. will be conducted to better understand the nature and extent of the decline. It should be noted that the osprey population in the lower Columbia River and Willamette River have been producing around 1.5 to 1.6 young per occupied nest (Henny et. al. 2008). These populations have shown large population increases in recent years.

If declines are detected, the UCBN in conjunction with the resource management staff at LARO will discuss causes of these declines, including consideration of natural population cycles, weather, productivity, contaminants, changes in fish distribution or abundance, habitat changes or any other significant evidence. The result of the discussion will be to determine if the population of ospreys at LARO warrants expanded monitoring, or some additional research. At the end of each 5-year interval in monitoring we will conduct a trend analysis and submit a 5-year status and trend report.

Summary of the Benefits of the Selected Design
- The design directly reflects the study objectives.
- Using helicopter surveys every 3 years is an efficient method for monitoring all established nest sites and increases the likelihood of encountering newly occupied sites. Helicopter survey information will provide pertinent information to park management for the entire population of known and accessible osprey nests at LARO.
- The availability of GPS technology combined with high visitation at LARO creates an opportunity to engage volunteers and park staff in monitoring occupied nests from year-to-year.
- Measured covariates at occupied nest sites will assist in the interpretation of spatial and temporal patterns of osprey population density.
- The field techniques are easy to learn and use.

Field Methods

Field Season Preparations and Field Schedule

The first task is to revise procedures based on the experiences and results from the previous year. After any revisions are completed, preparation involves reviewing last year's data and adding any new nest site locations, gathering equipment, and fulfilling permitting and compliance requirements. Permits for LARO will be provided through the NPS research permit and reporting system (http://science.nature.nps.gov/research/ac/ResearchIndex). GPS devices will be loaded with all known osprey nest site locations before the start of each survey. Batteries and spare batteries must be charged for all GPS units, including backup units. Paper data entry forms will be updated and photocopied. SOPs should be thoroughly reviewed by directing staff well in advance of training and field work.

Arrangements must be made by February each year for issuing a contract for helicopter rental if an aerial survey is scheduled. Refer to SOP #9 for details on obtaining the services of a helicopter and pilot. Equipment needs are relatively modest, and once 2 pairs of image stabilization binoculars and sufficient GPS units are purchased, replacement will be infrequent.

If ground-based surveys are scheduled, arrangements must be made in coordination with LARO staff if boat or housing assistance is required. Equipment needs are relatively modest, and once sufficient binoculars and GPS units are purchased, replacement will be infrequent. An equipment list is included in SOP # 1. Special vehicle needs posed by this protocol include a vehicle with a towing capacity of at least 4,000 lbs. to tow a boat and trailer. Prior arrangements should be made with the resource manager at LARO for the use of a boat or a towing vehicle.

Locating and Observing Nest Activity

Helicopter Surveys

Helicopters used for osprey surveys will seat a pilot and 2 passengers. Observation of nestlings is easier with the doors off the helicopter. In order to avoid observer fatigue, the pilot should plan on landing and taking 15-20 minute breaks every 90 minutes or so during the course of the survey. The Project Leader must be aware of observer fatigue because a tired observer may not make accurate assessments of the occupancy of a nest or the number of young counted.

To facilitate maneuverability and control of the helicopter it is advised to approach nests into the wind when possible. During the productivity survey, one observer will keep watch on the location of adult birds while the other observer will record nestling numbers. Always approach a nest structure so you remain in full sight of the incubating bird. During all survey flights, approach known nests slowly (≤ 30 kilometers per hour) and maintain at least 300 m between the helicopter and the nest. Avoid hovering directly over the nest to minimize the potential of flushing the osprey from the nest.

Once an observer has visually located a nest structure, they should instruct the pilot to slowly fly toward the nest until the observer can determine if the nest is occupied. If you observe an incubating adult/subadult on the nest, ask the pilot to slowly turn the helicopter away from the nest and leave the area immediately to minimize disturbance to the incubating osprey. If you do not observe an incubating osprey, look for other signs of occupation including nest building or territorial behavior (undulating, copulating, and vocalizing). Once you determine the status (occupied, unoccupied, etc.) of the nest, proceed with the survey to the next known nesting site or continue to scan the survey route for any new nest sites.

Record all information regarding the nest site on the field data forms (SOP # 9, Tables 8-9) or the survey map immediately after making observations. Be sure to complete information on survey times, landing locations, crew, pilot, aircraft (SOP #9, Table 10) and also record weather information for the day of the survey (SOP #9, Table 11). At the end of the day, summarize your survey results, and develop a strategy if additional helicopter time is needed to survey additional sections of the study area.

The "activity" survey in mid-May is complete after determining the status of all observed nests. The "productivity" is complete in mid-July after determining the number of young per occupied nests, identified from the activity survey.

Flight lines will be designated for the triennial helicopter survey so that all areas without 1500m of the reservoir are searched for new nest sites. The helicopter pilot will be instructed at the beginning of the survey that it is important to locate new nest sites as well as document nesting activity at nest sites occupied during previous data collection efforts. An effort will be made to detect as many new nest sites as possible by helicopter.

Ground-based Surveys
Driving directions to Lake Roosevelt are included in SOP # 4. Nest sites will be located using GPS waypoints, following procedures outlined in SOP # 3. Field crews will consist of teams of at least 2 people and each team will be assigned to a set of known nest sites and given a map, similar to Figure 2 and Appendix B-D, along with a set of GPS coordinates for each nest site (Appendix E). When a nest site is located team members will establish an observation point from which to watch the nest for signs of osprey activity. Field crews will systematically survey the whole area within 1500 m of each shoreline of the lake for nesting ospreys. This will include evaluating the old nests for occupancy during the initial survey each year or flight every 3 years, and locating other new nests.

Once on site, nest site observation is fairly straightforward. Spring and summer weather extremes can cause challenging conditions, and all team members must arrive prepared with warm clothes and rain gear, sun hats, and plenty of water. Before the start of each field session, nest locations will be organized into convenient and efficient routes through the study area, according to the number of field teams available. These routes will be illustrated on hard copy maps provided to each team. GPS units employed by the UCBN typically allow navigation accuracies of 1-3 m.

Crew training will occur in the field prior to each observation occasion under the direction of UCBN and/or park staff, as detailed in SOP # 2. Nest site characteristics will be recorded for each new nest added to the database during the initial spring survey once nest site occupancy is established (SOP #4).

Osprey NestWatch Volunteer Program

Beginning in 2010, volunteers and park management will be asked to participate in the "Lake Roosevelt NestWatch Program." The osprey observation program will assist UCBN project staff with details on annual osprey nest activity. Volunteers will be asked to visit their chosen nest(s) at least once every other week from May until the ospreys leave in late summer for their annual migration to southern Mexico. Ideally, volunteers should have identified a nest near their home or office, or be willing to drive to one often. Details for the start-up and close out to the Osprey NestWatch program each year are contained in SOP #10. Volunteers should have access to the internet to report their findings and to receive updates on what is happening with other nests around the lake.

Volunteer osprey monitors will receive an information package at the beginning of April each year with information on the "Lake Roosevelt NestWatch Program", links to the website, and other useful information. Volunteer observers will be asked to complete an online form, provided as a web link from the UCBN osprey vital sign webpage, to report nest site observations (http://science.nature.nps.gov/im/units/ucbn/monitor/osprey/osprey.cfm). Information included in the online observation form includes: nest site name, survey date, observer name and phone number, survey method (ground/vehicle or boat), number of adults observed, number of nestlings observed, and osprey behavior observed (e.g., adult in incubation posture, adult feeding young, adult bringing food to nest, etc.).

Because UCBN nest surveys are conducted only twice during the breeding season, once during nest initiation and incubation and once to count chicks, volunteers will assist in the collection of additional observations on a more frequent basis for a subset of nests. These additional observations will be added to the overall database but do not replace the annual activity or productivity survey conducted by UCBN field crews. Nest information from the osprey NestWatch program will be entered directly into an Access database and this information will be merged at the end of the season with the information obtained by UCBN survey crews.

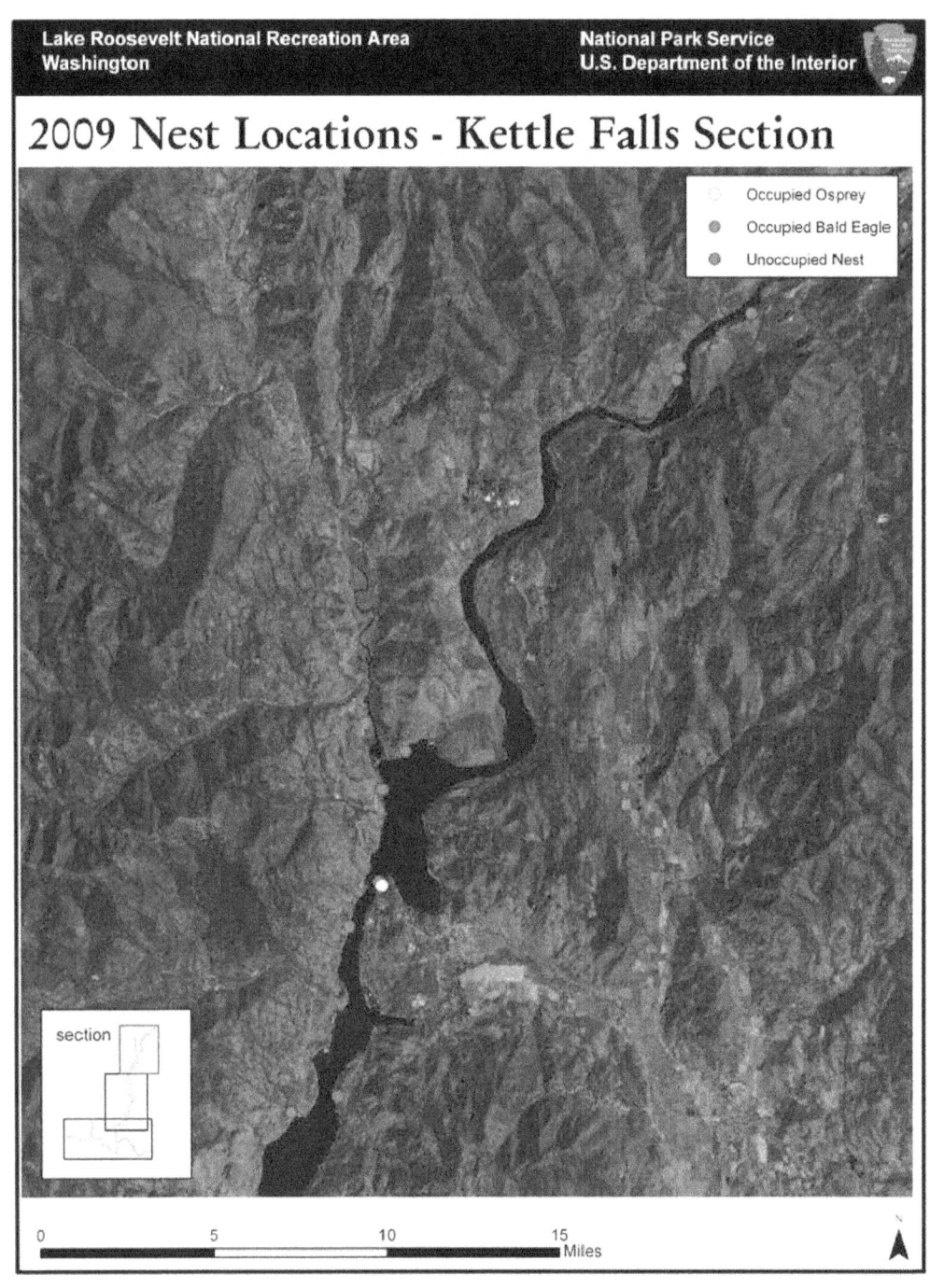

Figure 2. Locations of osprey nest sites during 2009 survey along the Kettle Falls Section of LARO.

Data Entry and Management

Pilot osprey data in 2007-2009 were collected with paper forms. Paper data sheets make it much easier to prevent data loss and their use facilitates participation by volunteers in the entire field process. This protocol version is designed around the use of paper data sheets and internet access for capturing volunteer observer information.

Paper data entry is relatively straightforward, and data sheet templates are included in SOP # 9 – Tables 7-10 for helicopter surveys, and Appendix 1-2 of the SOP document for ground-based activity and productivity surveys. The basic structure involves a document with discrete choices for observers to record nest site activity. Data sheets, with known nest site GPS coordinates and nest site photos, will be prepared for each field team prior to entry into the field. Blank spreadsheets will be available to accommodate any addition of new nest site locations.

The preferred order of field operations and data entry steps are as follows:
1. Locate nest site
2. Record species
3. Record GPS coordinates and nest site location (if this is a new nest site location)
4. Record nest site observations
5. Record nest site characteristics (if this is a new nest site)
6. Take a nest site photo (if this is a new nest site location)
7. Add any necessary comments in the "notes" column
8. Review data entry before moving to the next nest site location

Data sheets will be inspected by team leaders and the project leader at the end of each field day, as a key step in the quality assurance and quality control process (QA/QC). Data entry from paper forms into the working copy of the osprey project database (a Microsoft Access database, described in detail in SOP # 5) will be performed by UCBN staff or volunteer(s) in an office setting after completion of field work, and will also be treated as an additional opportunity to conduct QA/QC. Validation rules programmed into the database will help detect logical inconsistencies, such as out of range data (e.g. 20 osprey young, instead of 2 osprey young). Paper data sheets will be archived by the UCBN on a short-term basis only, up to 3 years, which will allow sufficient time for all possible QA/QC problems to be resolved. The UCBN will maintain the master database as the official record of protocol data, following procedures established in the UCBN Data Management Plan (Dicus and Garrett 2007) to ensure the master database is properly archived and remains compatible with applicable software.

After the Field Season

Following field work, equipment should be stored in the UCBN headquarters. Currently most equipment is stored at the UCBN headquarters in Moscow, ID, but this may change if LARO resource staff begins to take on more responsibility in planning and implementing field work with SCA interns. Electronic equipment, including GPS units, should have the batteries removed during winter months to prevent corrosion and leaking, and will be stored in plastic bins in the UCBN office. All osprey waypoints, which are temporary for a single season, should be deleted from GPS units at the end of each field season prior to winter storage. Data entry should begin as soon as possible in order to address outstanding QA/QC problems before memories fade and personnel change.

Data Handling, Analysis, and Reporting

While the following section outlines procedures for osprey data handling, analysis, and report development, additional details and context for this chapter may be found in the UCBN Data Management Plan (Dicus and Garrett 2007), which describes the overall information management strategy for the network. The UCBN monitoring plan also provides a good overview of the Network's information management and reporting plan (Garrett et al. 2007).

Overview of Database Design

A customized relational database application, implemented in Microsoft Access, has been designed to store and manipulate the data associated with this project. The design of this database is consistent with NPS I&M Natural Resource Database Template version 3.2 and UCBN standards (NPS 2007). The database will continue to undergo revisions, which will be reflected in both this protocol narrative and the data management SOP. The general database strategy is to use a blank version of the protocol database (a "working copy") to enter, error-check, and validate a given season's data, then migrate that data to the read-only "master version" of the protocol database. This strategy protects validated data from corruption, and the master version will facilitate multi-year analyses. The underlying data structure (tables, fields, and relationships) will always remain the same in both versions, and they will have very similar front-end database applications ("user interface" with forms, queries, etc.) accessed through a user-friendly "switchboard" (Figure 3). The user interface of the working copy database will serve data entry, quality control, and validation needs. The user interface of the master database application will serve analysis and summarization needs, including specific reporting and exporting format needs. Details of the database, including a description of core and peripheral tables and a logical model of table relationships, are presented in SOP # 5.

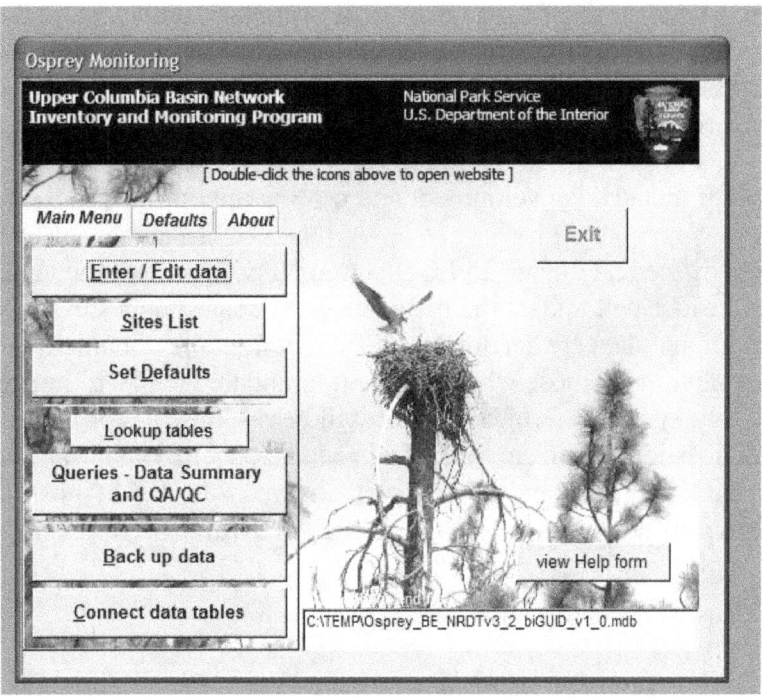

Figure 3. Draft version of the UCBN osprey monitoring project database user interface.

Data Entry

Entry of data from paper field sheets to the database will be accomplished each season shortly after completion of field work. The database's data entry form resembles the layout of the paper field sheet, and has built-in quality assurance components such as pick lists and validation rules to test for missing data or illogical combinations. Data entry is viewed as an important step in the overall QA/QC process, and care should be taken to review both the input from the paper forms and the resulting entries in the database.

Quality Review

After the data have been entered and processed, all data will be reviewed by the Project Leader for quality, completeness, and logical consistency. The working database application will facilitate this process by showing the results of pre-built queries that check for data integrity, data outliers and missing values, and illogical values. The user may then fix these problems and document the fixes. If all errors and inconsistencies cannot be fixed, the resulting errors will be documented and included in the metadata and certification report.

Metadata Procedures

Data documentation is a critical step toward ensuring that datasets are useable for their intended purposes well into the future. This involves the development of metadata, which can be defined as structured information about the content, quality, and condition of data. Additionally, metadata provide the means to catalog datasets within intranet and internet systems, making data available to a broad range of potential users. Metadata for all UCBN monitoring data will conform to Federal Geographic Data Committee (FGDC) and NPS guidelines and will contain all components of supporting information such that the data may be confidently manipulated, analyzed, and synthesized. For long-term projects such as this one, metadata creation is most time consuming the first time it is developed – after which most information remains static from one year to the next. Metadata records in subsequent years then only need to be updated to reflect current publications, references, taxonomic conventions, contact information, data disposition and quality, and to describe any changes in collection methods, analysis approaches, or quality assurance for the project.

Specific procedures for metadata development and posting are outlined in the UCBN Data Management Plan. In general, the Project Leader and the Data Manager (or Data Technician) will work together to create and update an FGDC- and NPS-compliant metadata record in XML format. The Project Leader will update the metadata content as changes to the protocol are made, and each year as additional data are accumulated. Edits within the document will be tracked so that any changes are obvious to those who will use it to update the XML metadata file. At the conclusion of the field season, the Project Leader will be responsible for providing a completed, up-to-date metadata questionnaire form to the Data Manager. The Data Manager will facilitate metadata development by creating and parsing metadata records, and by posting such records to national clearinghouses as described below (See Data Archival Procedures).

Sensitive Information

Part of metadata development includes determining whether or not the data include any sensitive information, which includes specific locations of rare, threatened, or endangered species. Prior to completing metadata, the Project Leader and Park Resource Manager will work together to identify any sensitive information in the data. Their findings will be documented and communicated to the Data Manager. Sensitive information is not being collected in the osprey monitoring program at this time.

Data Certification and Delivery

Data certification is a benchmark in the project information management process that indicates 1) the data are complete for the period of record; 2) they have undergone and passed the quality assurance / quality control (QA/QC) checks; and 3) that they are appropriately documented and in a condition for archiving, posting, and distribution. Certification is not intended to imply that the data are completely free of errors or inconsistencies which may not have been detected during QA/QC reviews.

To ensure that only data of the highest possible quality are included in reports and other project deliverables, the data certification step is an annual requirement for all tabular and spatial data. The Project Leader is primarily responsible for completing certification. The completed form, certified data, and updated metadata will be delivered to the Data Manager according to table 6 in the Operational Requirements section. Additional details of the certification and delivery processes are included in SOP # 6.

Data Analysis

Annual Status Summary

Status results will be summarized after each year of data collection. Standard summary information will be presented for nesting ospreys at LARO with content similar to that shown in Tables 3 and 4, and will include the number of nests checked, number of occupied nests, number of osprey young, and average number of young per occupied nest. A summary of nest tree characteristics (means and standard errors) will also be provided for occupied nest trees. Nest tree characteristics reported will include: nest height (m), tree height (m), tree diameter at breast height (cm), distance to water (m), species of tree, and height and diameter of the 4 nearest trees that reach at least the lower canopy height of the nest tree (Edwards and Collopy 1988).

Table 4. Example of annual summary information for the LARO osprey population.

Results of Osprey Survey	2009
Number of Nest Sites Checked	9
Number of Occupied Nests	4
Number of Osprey Young	6
Average Number of Osprey Young per Occupied Nest	1.5

Trend Analysis

After 5 years of data collection (2 years of helicopters surveys and 3 years of ground-based surveys), evidence of change in the two key metrics of number of nests occupied and number of fledglings per occupied nest will be evaluated with the non-parametric Mann-Kendall test, which uses a simple rank-based correlation coefficient, Kendall's tau, to determine if nest occupancy is correlated with time (Helsel and Hirsch 1991, Higgins 2004). Simple summaries will be made with the multi-year averages, as shown in Table 4. A table similar to Table 4 will be generated for the LARO 5-year annual status and trend report.

Table 5. Breeding success of Ospreys in the West Kootenay during 2006, compared to the nine-year average and range of values for 1997-2005 (Arndt 2007).

Indicators of Breeding Success	2006	1997-2005 mean (range)
Number of occupied nests	27	34 (21-56)
Number of young	29	44 (15-96)
No. young per occupied nest	1.07	1.23 (0.71 – 1.71)

Graphical tools will also be used to display biologically important changes in osprey numbers and productivity over time. For example, a simple line graph of a time series of occupied nest counts can be effective. Figure 4. illustrates a simulated trend of a 50% decline in osprey nest occupancy over 20 years, with a stochastic component introduced by drawing from a binomial error distribution, provides a realistic illustration of how osprey observation data may be presented over time. The dashed line represents a Poisson regression line (for count data) fitted to the nest counts over time. In this example, the estimated annual rate of decline was 3.4%. The estimated correlation coefficient τ between the number of occupied nests and year was -0.53 (p=0.002). This figure was drawn from one iteration of our power analysis simulation described previously, showing how nest counts may vary from year to year, but also show an overall trend. A generalized linear model using a log-linear transformation suitable for counts (i.e., a "Poisson" error structure) was plotted over this time series to illustrate our approach to obtaining an overall estimate of mean trend over time. See SOP #6 for more details.

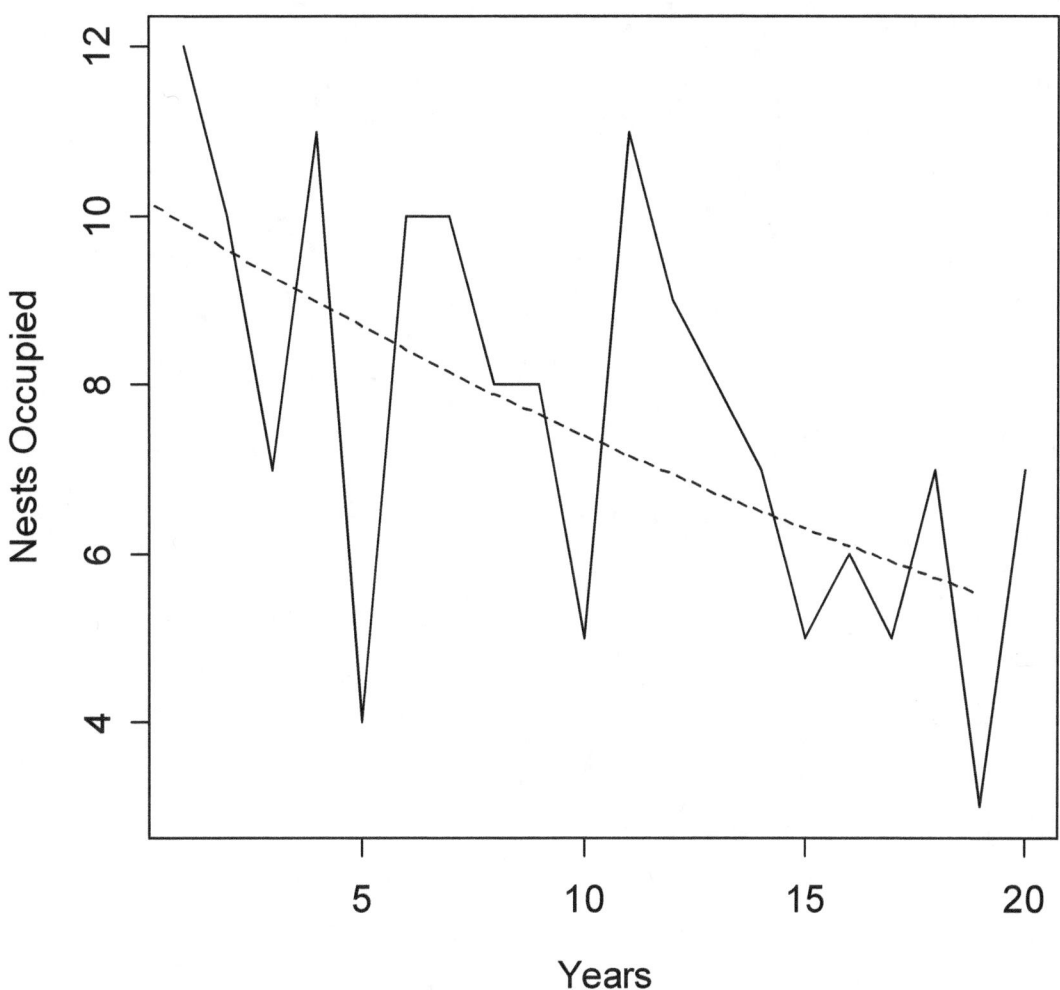

Figure 4. A simulated trend of nest occupancy.

Reporting

A summary will be produced annually, with a more detailed status and trend report produced every 5 years. The annual summary will:

- List project personnel and their roles.
- List nest site locations and observations recorded during the current year.
- Provide a summary history of the number of occupied nests and productivity as measured by the number of young per occupied nest.
- Provide status and trend (after 2014) estimates for the osprey population at LARO.
- Provide a summary of additional nest tree characteristics, including mean nest height (m), tree height (m), tree DBH, distance to water (m), and species of tree.
- Provide map(s) of annual nest site locations.
- Evaluate data quality and identify any data quality concerns and/or deviations from protocols that affect data quality and interpretability.
- Evaluate and identify suggested or required changes to the protocol.

The annual summary will be developed and formatted according to the natural resource report series template for natural resource technical reports with instructions located at http://www.nature.nps.gov/publications/NRPM/index.cfm. A 1-2 page resource brief will be prepared for public consumption, and provided to park interpretive staff for distribution to interested visitors. A template for the resource brief is included in SOP # 6. An NPS template for producing maps with ESRI ArcGIS or ArcView software is available at http://imgis.nps.gov/templates.html.

Osprey nest site locations will be reported to the LARO resource managers as early in the nesting season as possible. Reported information will include GPS locations and location maps so that resource managers can direct boat vehicle traffic or visitors away from a nest site, if necessary.

A more in-depth status and trend analysis and report will be produced approximately every 5 years, or as the importance of emerging information warrants. This report will provide greater analytical and interpretive detail, and will evaluate the relevance of findings to long-term management goals. The report should also evaluate operational aspects of the monitoring program, such as whether the observation period remains appropriate. The timing of the spring arrival of birds at the nest site could conceivably change over time in response to climate change.

The 5-year status and trend report will use the NPS Natural Resource Publications Natural Resource Technical Report (NRTR) template, a pre-formatted Microsoft Word template document based on current NPS formatting standards. This template, guidelines for its use and documentation of the NPS publication standards are available at the following address: http://www.nature.nps.gov/publications/NRPM/index.cfm. This osprey protocol is also an excellent example of the NPS Natural Resource Report formatting standard, which is very similar to the NRTR template.

Data Archival Procedures

Paper data sheets will be archived for 3 years, which allow ample time to complete QA/QC and certification steps for digital data. Long-term archiving will only be used for digital data.

Once the annual data certification has been completed, the UCBN Osprey database and related UCBN reports will be archived on the UCBN server, posted to the UCBN website, and posted to the national web-accessible secure Integrated Resource Management Application (IRMA) hosted by the NPS Washington Areas Support Office (WASO) or National I&M program. The IRMA application incorporates functionality previously handled by separate databases into a single web interface that comprises:

- The master database for natural resource bibliographic references
- The master database for biodiversity information including species occurrences and physical or written evidence for the occurrence (i.e., references, vouchers, and observations)
- A centralized data repository with a graphical search interface.

A review of archive and expendable data products will be undertaken by the Project Lead and Data Manager during season close-out each year. An example of an expendable data product is an intermediate draft of an annual report that was saved during report preparation.

Protocol Testing and Revision

The draft version (version 1.0) of this protocol was developed and tested in 2009. Subsequent protocol testing will occur during each field season and evaluation of existing protocols and recommended revisions will be documented in annual reports and during season close-out.

Revisions to this protocol and the SOPs will be documented by version numbers in the change history on page iii. We anticipate there may be revisions to the detailed instructions to field crews. Additional SOPs added in the future may include methods for collection of feathers for testing of contaminants or collection of prey items for analysis. Population boundaries will be revised only if osprey distributions and management priorities shift significantly, and should be done only in consultation with park management and careful consideration of statistical consequences. Analytical techniques may change, particularly if statistical distributions change in shape such that other parametric tools can offer more power in trend detection. This possibility should be considered and evaluated frequently with goodness-of-fit tests. All revisions will be carefully documented using the protocol development and revision log in SOP # 7 and the change history log at the front of each SOP and this narrative.

Personnel Requirements and Training

Personnel Requirements

This monitoring project requires, at a minimum, participation and leadership from the UCBN Coordinator/Project Leader and the Network Data Manager, and a biotech who is a skilled field team leader and can provide expertise in field operations. The roles and responsibilities outlined in Table 6 of this protocol can be provided by these 3 individuals. However, additional assistance from park staff will ease the annual workload generated by this effort and ensure a high quality information product. This monitoring effort is unique in its emphasis on participation by volunteers, and, assuming that we can sustain this participation over time, additional professional personnel are not necessary. The UCBN Volunteers-In-Parks (VIP) program coordinator must also participate in the organization and supervision of citizen science volunteers. Currently the UCBN communication specialist is serving as a VIP coordinator for network activities, and is supported by the LARO VIP coordinator for this particular project (SOP #10). Volunteers must be provided a job description, given identifying t-shirts and/or hats, and signed up with the appropriate VIP forms (including parental approval forms for minors). Volunteer hours accumulated during osprey field work will be included in the UCBN (10-150) year-end VIP report. Details on the UCBN volunteer program are included in SOP #10.

The field crew will consist of the Project Leader and a UCBN biotech and/or a seasonal Student Conservation Association (SCA) intern from LARO. Field assistants must be able to work outdoors, learn GPS and data entry, and identify ospreys. Project Leaders and biotech's must have these skills, and an understanding of project objectives and experience with field work and GPS. During 2 years of pilot work conducted during the development of this protocol, we successfully trained and used SCAs to collect field data. We will actively pursue this approach to sustain this monitoring effort in the future. Data management staff must be able to handle the described GPS/GIS and database tasks. The Project Leader will conduct the described annual summaries, power analyses, and trend analyses.

Experience during the 2008 and 2009 field seasons provided a good estimate of staff time required for field sampling. In 2008, observations were completed at 13 osprey nests and 17 eagle nests with 1 team in 7 full days. The entire team consisted of a LARO biotech and a SCA intern. Based on this experience, we expect that a typical team will be able to accomplish adequate training and complete observations at 30 nests in 7 days. This protocol will require approximately 2 weeks of field time annually. One week in mid-May to determine occupancy of established nest sites and survey for new nest sites and one week in mid-July to determine the number of young fledged at occupied nest sites. A few additional days may be required if the weather limits nest site observations or if the number of young cannot be determined on the first visit to the nest site in July. Once several years of data have been collected, the addition of nest sites from year-to-year will probably be limited, due to the annual availability of additional new nest site trees or structures. The population of nesting ospreys is limited to available nesting trees or structures, which are not increasing substantially from year-to-year.

We are incorporating a strong citizen science and/or volunteer component to this protocol. The UCBN data manager, in cooperation with the Project Leader and VIP coordinator, designed a webpage for the "Osprey NestWatch Program" which was launched in April 2010. LARO staff and volunteers will find information on this website about the NestWatch program objectives, ecological background on ospreys, and a weblink to online data collection tools. It is our expectation that the information delivered through the Osprey NestWatch program will increase public and staff appreciation and understanding for the natural resources at LARO.

Roles and Responsibilities

Table 6. Roles and responsibilities for implementing the UCBN osprey monitoring program. Current or anticipated staff and volunteers for 2010 are named here.

Role	Responsibilities	Name / Position
Project Leader	• Project oversight and administration • Track project objectives, budget, requirements, and progress toward meeting objectives • Facilitate communications between NPS and cooperator(s) • Coordinate and ratify changes to protocol • Plan and execute field visits • Assist in training and safety instruction of field crews • Acquire and maintain field equipment • Perform data summaries and analyses • Maintain and archive project records • Project operations and implementation • Oversee data collection and entry, verify accurate data transcription into database • Complete an annual field season report • Certify each season's data for quality and completeness • Complete reports, metadata, and other products according to schedule	UCBN Program Manager or designated UCBN ecologist/biologist
Field Team Leader (BioTech)	• Collect, record, enter and verify data	UCBN Biotech, SCA Intern, Volunteer, Citizen Scientist (need only 1 person to fulfill this role)
Data Manager	• Consultant on data management activities • Facilitate check-in, review and posting of data, metadata, reports, and other products to national databases and clearinghouses according to schedule • Maintain and update database application • Provide database training as needed • Consultant on GPS use • Work with the project leader to analyze spatial data and develop metadata for spatial data products • Primary steward of Access database and GIS data and products	UCBN Data Manager
Park Resource Manager	• Consultant on all phases of protocol implementation • Facilitate boat logistics planning and coordination • Communicate management plans and associated information to the project leader • Review reports, data, and other project deliverables	LARO Resource Manager

Training and Calibration

All team members will train together. At the start of each field season, the Project Leader will train crews in the field during the annual "activity" survey and again during the "productivity" survey. Under the guidance of an experienced team leader, each team will practice locating GPS points and correctly filling in an osprey nest monitoring datasheet. Experience in 2008 and 2009 leads us to believe this can be accomplished during 1 morning of training, with the caveat being that all nest site observers have received some preliminary exposure to the project by being given copies of the protocol and SOPs to read prior to field training.

Operational Requirements

Annual Workload and Schedule

The annual workload of this monitoring program is outlined in Table 6 of the preceding section on Roles and Responsibilities. Table 6 provides a good overview of the general roles and tasks (responsibilities) required to complete all aspects of this program following rigorous and comprehensive information management practices as outlined by the UCBN Data Management Plan (Dicus and Garrett 2007). The budget in Table 9 demonstrates that adequate resources have been allocated to data management, analysis, and reporting activities. The SOPs provide a comprehensive step-by-step description of the annual workload and tasks required for completion, including data management tasks and product delivery. Annual preparation for osprey monitoring begins in January with the arrangement for helicopter surveys, boats and/or lodging at LARO for the mid-May activity survey. Recruitment of volunteer citizen scientists begins earnestly in April each year but park staff will be kept informed of the Osprey NestWatch program year-round through the UCBN bi-annual newsletter and attendance by UCBN staff at LARO park meetings. An evaluation of the protocol and any necessary changes must be made by April each year. Field work commences in mid-May, and data entry and QA/QC procedures begin immediately in August after the second nest site visits are completed. Table 7 provides additional details of the annual schedule.

Citizen Science / Volunteer Partnerships

It is worth underscoring the importance of planning for citizen science or volunteer participation as early as possible before the field season, and certainly no later than April preceding spring field work. Network and park staff will coordinate closely on this, determine primary contacts for outreach with outside volunteer organizations, and solicit commitments and schedules well in advance from interested groups.

Table 7. Annual schedule of major tasks and events for the UCBN osprey monitoring protocol.

Month	Administration	Field	Data Management/Reporting
January	UCBN annual report and work plan complete, Begin recruiting and hiring if a biotech needs to be hired. Arrange for helicopter survey and / or boat and lodging at LARO for mid-May activity survey		
February	Administer and modify existing agreements, if necessary	Provide GPS and other training to UCBN and park staff as needed	
March		Prepare maps, field data sheets, and GPS equipment	
April		Begin recruiting volunteers	
May		Activity survey - make first visits to existing nest sites to observe activity (mid-May) and record any new nest sites.	
June		Volunteers begin to send in observation reports	Data entry and verification from the mid-May activity survey
July		Productivity survey - make second nest site visit to observe number of young produced per occupied nest (mid-July). Follow-up nest site visit for productivity of late-nesting birds, if necessary (late-July).	
August			Data entry and verification from the mid-July productivity survey
September			Preliminary analysis of current year's results, Annual resource brief prepared for UCBN Science Advisory Committee meeting
October	UCBN annual report and work plan drafted. Budget preparation for new fiscal year	Field season report complete	Metadata production, quality review. Data certification complete; Data archival and posting
November			Analysis, reporting, and close-out
December			Close-out complete

Equipment Needs

Equipment needs are modest for this protocol. The list of equipment is included in Table 8. GPS units need to be maintained and replaced, if necessary, during the late winter/early spring well in advance of field season. A LARO-maintained NPS boat (Figure 5) equipped with all necessary state and federally regulated safety equipment including life preservers, flares, fire extinguisher, lights, etc. is available to the osprey monitoring crew and arrangements need to be made in January/February with the LARO resource manager for using this boat. The Project Leader has taken the NPS Motorboat Operator Certification Course and is qualified to operate this boat. Additional UCBN staff may be asked to take the Motorboat Operator training depending on annual needs. LARO has limited housing options but local motel arrangements can be made in Coulee Dam or Kettle Falls to accommodate field crews.

Table 8. Equipment list for monitoring osprey nests at LARO.

Observation Equipment	Navigation and Recording Equipment	Safety Equipment
Binoculars	GPS units	2-way radios
Hard copies of SOPs	PDA or weatherized data entry forms	First aid kit
Digital camera	Backup copies of data forms	Boat safety equipment
Guidebook to the identification of ospreys	Mechanical pencils and clip boards	Water, sunglasses, sunscreen
Maps of nest site locations from previous year	Clinometer (nest site characteristics)	
	DBH Tape (nest site characteristics)	
	Compass	
	Rangefinder (nest site characteristics)	

Figure 5. Photo of the 17 foot 90 horsepower Hewescraft boat, located at LARO, available for osprey monitoring.

Budget

Table 9. Detailed 2010 annual budget for osprey monitoring in the UCBN.

UCBN Osprey Monitoring Budget	Time allotted	% of time spent on DM*	Cost in dollars DM*	Cost in dollars (2009)
Expenditures				
Permanent NPS Personnel				
Program Manager (GS12) and Project Leader	Project Coordination: 1 week prep for sampling, 2 weeks sampling, 2 weeks data analysis and report	35%	$3,500	$10,000
Data Manager (GS11)	1 week database management, 1 week data archiving	100%	$3,400	$3,400
Seasonal Personnel				
BioTech	2 weeks sampling, 1 week data input and QA/QC	35%	$1,050	$3,000
Park Personnel				
Interpretive Staff	2 weeks school group recruiting and training			In-Kind support
Resource Management Staff	1 week resource management support (SCA interns)			In-Kind support
Volunteers (Citizen Scientists)				
NPS Staff and Volunteers	30 additional hours of observation (10 volunteers X 30 minutes/day X 6 days)			In-Kind support
Operations/Equipment				
GPS units ($450.00/unit)***	4 units			$1,800
Rangefinder Binoculars*** ($2,000/unit)	2 units			$4,000
NPS Boat (LARO)				In-Kind support
Travel (permanent employees)				$2,000
Other (contingency)				$500
Helicopter survey (every 3 years)	16 hours flight time			$15,000****
TOTAL			$7,950**	$24,700

* DM = data management
** More than 30% of the osprey protocol budget is dedicated to data management, analysis, and reporting activities.
*** Start-up expenses for equipment (not recurring).
****Not included in annual budget total (recurring every 3 years)

Literature Cited

Ames, P. L. 1966. DDT residues in the eggs of the osprey in the Northeastern United States and their relation to nesting success. Supplement: pesticides in the environment and their effects on wildlife. The Journal of Applied Ecology 3:87-97.

Arndt, J. 2007. Osprey monitoring in the West Kootenay Region: Results from 2006. British Columbia Birds 16:20-23.

Baldwin, C. M., J. G. McLellan, M. C. Polacek, and K. Underwood. 2003. Walleye predation on hatchery releases of kokanees and rainbow trout in Lake Roosevelt, Washington. North American Journal of Fisheries Management 23:660-676.

Bent, A.C. 1937. Life histories of North American birds of prey, Part 1. U.S. National Museum Publication 167. Washington, DC.

Bildstein, K. L. 2001. Why migratory birds of prey make great biological indicators. PP. 169-179 *in* K.L. Bildstein and D. Klem, Jr. (eds.), Hawkwatching in the Americas. Hawk Migration Association of America, North Wales, PA.

Bonar, S. A., L. G. Brown, P. E. Mongillo, and K. Williams. 2000. Biology, distribution and management of burbot (*Lota lota*) in Washington state. Northwest Science 74:87-96.

Carrier, W. D. and W .E. Melquist. 1976. The use of a rotor-winged aircraft in conducting nesting surveys of ospreys in northern Idaho. Raptor Research 10(3):77-83.

D'Eon, R. G. and W. R. Watt. 1994. Osprey management guidelines in Northeastern Ontario: a review. TR-018. Minnesota Natural Resources, Northeast Science and Technology, Timmins, ON.

Dicus, G. H. and L. K. Garrett. 2007. Upper Columbia Basin Network Data Management Plan. National Park Service Upper Columbia Basin Network Inventory and Monitoring Program. Moscow, ID.

Edwards, T. C. and M. W. Collopy. 1988. Nest tree preference of osprey in Northcentral Florida. J. Wildl. Manage. 52(1):109-107.

Elliott, J.E., M. M. Machmer, C. J. Henny, L. K. Wilson, and R. J. Norstrom. 1998. Contaminants in ospreys from the Pacific Northwest: I. Trends and patterns in polychlorinated dibenzo-p-dioxins and dibenzofurans in eggs and plasma. Arch Environ Contam Toxicol 35:620–631.

Elliott, J.E., M. M. Machmer, L. K. Wilson, and C. J. Henny. 2000. Contaminants in ospreys from the Pacific Northwest: II. Organochlorine pesticides, polychlorinated biphenyls and mercury, 1991–1997. Arch Environ Contam Toxicol 38:93–106.

Elliott, J.E., L. K. Wilson, C. J. Henny, S. F. Trudeau, F. A. Leighton, S. W. Kennedy, and K. M. Cheng. 2001. Assessment of biological effects of chlorinated hydrocarbons in osprey chicks. Environ Toxicol Chem 20:866–879.

Energy Northwest. 2005. Bald Eagle and Osprey Nest Survey Study Plan for Energy Northwest's Packwood Lake Hydroelectric Project FERC No. 2244 Lewis County, Washington. Bellingham, WA.

Environmental Protection Agency. 2006. Phase I sediment sampling data evaluation, Upper Columbia River site. CERCLA RI/FS. Prepared by Ecology and Environment, Inc. Hawkwatching in the Americas, 169-179.

Ewins, P. J. 1997. Osprey (*Pandion haliaetus*) populations in forested areas of North America: Changes, their causes and management recommendations. J. Raptor Res. 31:138–150.

Garrett, L. K., T. J. Rodhouse, G. H. Dicus, C. C. Caudill, and M. R. Shardlow. 2007. Upper Columbia Basin Network vital signs monitoring plan. Natural Resource Report NPS/UCBN/NRR—2007/002. National Park Service, Fort Collins, CO.

Gerrodette, T. 1987. A power analysis for detecting trends. Ecology 68:1364-1372.

Grove, R.A., C.J. Henny, and J.L. Kaiser. 2009. Osprey: Worldwide sentinel species for assessing and monitoring environmental contamination in rivers, lakes, reservoirs, and estuaries. J. Toxicol and Environ. Health, Part B. 12:25-44.

Helsel, D. R. and R. M. Hirsch. 1991. Statistical methods in water resources: Techniques of water-resources investigations of the United States. Geological Survey Book 4: Hydrologic analysis and interpretation, Chapter A3, Reston, VA.

Henny, C. J. 2005. An assessment of the status of nesting Ospreys and waterbirds along Lake Roosevelt with special emphasis toward future contaminant studies. Unpublished Research proposal.

Henny, C.J., J.A. Collins, and W.J. Deibert. 1978. Osprey distribution, abundance, and status in western North America: II. The Oregon population. Murrelet 59(1) 14-25. Available from http://wdfw.wa.gov/wlm/diversty/soc/state_monitor.htm (accessed 23 June 2009).

Henny, C.J., R.A. Grove, and J.L. Kaiser. 2008. Osprey distribution, abundance, reproductive status and contaminant burdens along the lower Columbia River, 1997/1998 versus 2004. Arch. Environ. Contam. Toxicol. 54:525-534.

Henny, C.J., R. A. Grove, J. L. Kaiser, and V. R. Bentley. 2004. An evaluation of osprey eggs to determine spatial residue patterns and effects of contaminants along the lower Columbia River, USA. In: Chancellor RD, Meyburg BY (eds). Raptors Worldwide, WWGBP/MME, Budapest, Hungary, pp 369–388.

Henny, C.J. and J. L. Kaiser. 1996. Osprey population increase along the Willamette River, Oregon, and the role of utility structures, 1976–1993. In: Bird D. M., Varland, D. E., Negro J. J. (eds) Raptors in Human Landscapes. Academic, London, pp. 97–108.

Henny, C.J., J.L. Kaiser and R.A. Grove. 2009a. PCDDs, PCDFs, PCBs, OC pesticides and mercury in fish and osprey eggs from the Willamette River, Oregon (1993, 2001 and 2006) with calculated biomagnification factors. Ecotoxicology 18:151-173.

Henny, C.J., J.L. Kaiser, R.A. Grove, B.L. Johnson and R.J. Letcher. 2009b. Polybrominated diphenyl ether flame retardants in eggs may reduce reproductive success of ospreys in Oregon and Washington, USA. Ecotoxicology 18:802-813.

Henny, C.J., J.L. Kaiser, R.A. Grove, V.R. Bentley, and J.E. Elliott. 2003. Biomagnification factors (fish to osprey eggs from the Willamette River, Oregon, U.S.A.) for PCDDs, PCDFs, PCBs and OC pesticides. Environmental Monitoring and Assessment, 84(3):275-315.

Henny, C.J. and H.M. Wight. 1969. An endangered osprey population: Estimates of mortality and production. Auk 86:188-98.

Higgins, J. J. 2004. Introduction to modern nonparametric statistics. Brooks/Cole-Thomson Learning, Pacific Grove, CA.

Irwin, R. J. 2006. Draft Part B lite (Just the Basics) QA/QC Review Checklist for Aquatic Vital Sign Monitoring Protocols and SOPs, National Park Service, Water Resources Division. Fort Collins, CO. Available from http://www.nature.nps.gov/water/Vital_Signs_Guidance/Guidance_Documents/PartBLite.pdf (accessed 3 January 2010).

Johnson, D. R., W. E. Melquist, and T. L. Fleming. 2008. Rainstorm effects on osprey brood survival. J. Raptor Res. 42(1): 51-53.

Martell, M.S., Henny C.J., Nye P.E., Solensky M.J. 2001. Fall migration routes, timing, and wintering sites of North American ospreys as determined by satellite telemetry. Condor 103:715–724.

Melquist, W.E. 1974. Nesting success and chemical contamination in northern Idaho and northeastern Washington ospreys. Master's thesis. University of Idaho. Moscow, ID.

McLellan, H. J., J. G. McLellan, and A. T. Scholz. 2004. Evaluation of release strategies for hatchery kokanee in Lake Roosevelt, Washington. Northwest Science 78:158-167.

Morrison, L. W. 2007. Assessing the reliability of ecological monitoring data: power analysis and alternative approaches. Natural Areas Journal 27:83-91.

National Park Service (NPS). 1999. Natural resource challenge: the National Park Service's action plan for preserving natural resources. US Department of the Interior National Park Service, Washington, DC. Available from http://www.nature.nps.gov/challenge/challengedoc/index.htm (accessed 3 January 2010).

National Park Service (NPS). 2000. Lake Roosevelt National Recreation Area General Management Plan. US Department of the Interior, National Park Service, Washington, DC.

National Park Service (NPS). 2007. Natural Resource Database Template Version 3.2 documentation. Natural Resource Program Center, Office of Inventory, Monitoring, and Evaluation, Fort Collins, CO.

Oakley, K. L., L. P. Thomas, and S. G. Fancy. 2003. Guidelines for long-term monitoring protocols. Wildlife Society Bulletin 31:1000-1003.

Poole, A. F. 1989. Ospreys: A natural and unnatural history. Cambridge University Press.

Postupalsky, S. 1974. Raptor reproductive success: some problems with methods, criteria, and terminology. In: Hamerstrom, Jr. F.N., B.E. Harrell, and R.R. Olendroff (eds.) Management of Raptors. Raptor Research Foundation, Vermillion, SD, pp. 21–31.

Postupalsky, S. 1983. Techniques and terminology for surveys of nesting bald eagles. In: J.W. Grier, J.B. Elder, F.J. Gramlich, N.F. Green, J.V. Kussman, J.E. Mathisen, and J.P. Mattson (eds.) Northern states bald eagle recovery plan. US Fish and Wildlife Service, Twin Cities, MN, Appendix D.

Rahel, F. J. 2002. Homogenization of freshwater faunas. Annual Review of Ecology and Systematics 33:291-315.

Reese, J. G. 1972. Osprey nesting success along the Choptank River, Maryland. Chesapeake reflect regional differences in reproductive success. Journal of Wildlife Management 55:601-608.

Scholz, A. T., K. O'Laughlin, D. Geist, D. Peone, J. Uehara, L. Fields, T. Kleist, I. Zozaya, T. Peone and K. Teesatuskie. 1985. Compilation of information on salmon and steelhead total run size, catch and hydropower related losses in the Upper Columbia River Basin, above Grand Coulee Dam. Tech. Report No. 2. Upper Columbia United Tribes Fisheries. Coeur d'Alene, ID and Cheney, WA.

Steenhof, K. and I. Newton. 2007. Assessing nesting success and productivity. Pages 181-192 in Bird, D. M. and K. L. Bildstein. Raptor research and management techniques. Hancock House Publishers. Blaine, WA.

Steidl, R. J., C. R. Griffin, and L. J. Niles. 1991. Contaminant levels of osprey eggs and prey reflect regional differences in reproductive success. J. Wildl. Manage. 55:601–608.

Swenson, J.E. 1981. Osprey nest site characteristics in Yellowstone National Park. Journal of Field Ornithology. 52:67-69.

Titus, K., and M. R. Fuller. 1990. Recent trends in counts of migrant hawks from northeastern North America. J. Wildl. Manage. 54(3): 463-470.

US Geological Survey. 2003. Ospreys in Oregon and the Pacific Northwest. USGS FS-153-02, US Department of Interior, Washington, DC.

Vana-Miller, S.L. 1987. Habitat suitability index models: osprey. US Fish and Wildl. Serv. Biol. Rep. 82 (10.154).

Van Daele, L.J. and H.A. Van Daele. 1982. Factors affecting the productivity of ospreys nesting in west-central Idaho. Condor 84:292-299.

Washington Department Fish Wildlife (WDFW). 2009a. Priority habitat and species (PHS) list. Available from http://wdfw.wa.gov/hab/phspage.htm (accessed 8 August 2009).

Washington Department Fish Wildlife (WDFW) 2009b. Washington State Monitor List. Available from http://wdfw.wa.gov/wlm/diversty/soc/state_monitor.htm (accessed 8 August 2009).

Wiemeyer, S. N., D. M. Swineford, P. R. Spitzer, and P. D. McLain. 1978. Organochlorine residues in New Jersey osprey eggs. Bulletin of Environmental Contamination and Toxicology 19: 56-63.

Glossary of Terms Used by the UCBN I & M Program

Failed Nest is an occupied nest from which no young were fledged due to any cause including no eggs were laid, eggs were destroyed, eggs failed to hatch, or young hatched but died prior to fledging (Postupalsky 1974).

Fledge is the stage in a young bird's life when the feathers and wing muscles are sufficiently developed for flight. It also describes the act of raising chicks to a fully grown state by the chick's parents. A young bird that has recently fledged but is still dependent upon parental care and feeding is called a **fledgling**.

Logistic Regression is a form of regression analysis used to model binomial counts of 0-1, such as "occupied" and "unoccupied" nests. Logistic regression assumes the response variable Y has a binomial distribution, and the natural logarithm of the odds ratio (i.e. the logit transformation or "link function") of occupied to unoccupied nests (in our case) can be modeled by a linear combination of covariate parameters.

Mann-Kendall Test is a non-parametric test for correlation between a variable of interest such as occupied nest counts and time. The Kendall's τ ("tau") correlation coefficient is calculated by subtracting the number of concordant pairs (e.g., when both data points at time t are positive relative to data points at time t-1) and dividing this by the total number of pairs. The estimated correlation coefficient ranges from -1 to 1 and is interpreted the same as with Pearson's correlation coefficient r, where 1 indicates perfect positive association, -1 perfect negative correlation, and 0 indicates absence of correlation.

Occupied Nest is a nest with evidence of actual pairs (Postupalsky 1974).

Poisson Regression is a form of regression analysis used to model count data. Poisson regression assumes the response variable Y (e.g., occupied nest counts) has a Poisson distribution, and assumes the logarithm of its expected value (i.e., the mean value) can be modeled by a linear combination of unknown but fixed parameters (i.e., covariates). A Poisson regression model is sometimes known as a log-linear model.

Power analysis: The **power** of a statistical test is the probability that the test will reject a false null hypothesis, or in other words that it will not make a Type II error. As power increases, the chances of a Type II error decrease, and vice versa. The probability of a Type II error is referred to as β. Therefore power is equal to $1 - \beta$. Power is a function of effect size or minimum detectable change, variance of the parameter (e.g. standard error of the mean), and sample size. A power analysis determines the probability of correctly rejecting a false null hypothesis given fixed values of effect size, variance, and sample size.

Productivity is the number of young fledged per occupied nest. Productivity is calculated as the number of young produced divided by the total number of occupied nests (young/occupied nest).

Status is a measure of a current attribute, condition, or state, and is typically measured with population means.

Temporal variation is variation in a population parameter, such as a mean, over time. For our purposes this typically refers to variation seasonally or annually.

Trend is a measure of directional change over time and can occur in some population parameter, such as a mean (**net trend**), or in an individual member or unit of a population (**gross trend**).

Vital Signs are a subset of physical, chemical, and biological elements and processes of park ecosystems that are selected to represent the overall health or condition of park resources, known or hypothesized effects of stressors, or elements that have important human values. The elements and processes that are monitored are a subset of the total suite of natural resources that park managers are directed to preserve "unimpaired for future generations," including water, air, geological resources, plants and animals, and the various ecological, biological, and physical processes that act on those resources. Vital signs may occur at any level of organization including landscape, community, population, or genetic level, and may be compositional (referring to the variety of elements in the system), structural (referring to the organization or pattern of the system), or functional (referring to ecological processes).

Appendix A. Index of Standard Operating Procedures
(Bound as a separate volume)

SOP 1: Preparations for the Field Season
SOP 2: Training Observers and Osprey Identification
SOP 3: Finding GPS Waypoints
SOP 4: Measuring Nest Site Characteristics and Recording Nest Site Observations
SOP 5: Data Management
SOP 6: Data Summary, Analysis, and Reporting
SOP 7: Protocol Revision
SOP 8: Field Safety and Job Hazard Analysis
SOP 9: Aerial Surveys
SOP 10: Osprey Nest Watch Volunteer Program

This appendix is available from the Upper Columbia Basin Network website (http://www.nature.nps.gov/im/units/UCBN) and the Natural Resource Publications Management website (http://www.nature.nps.gov/publications/NRPM).

Appendix B. Map of nest site locations in LARO (2009 Coulee Dam section)

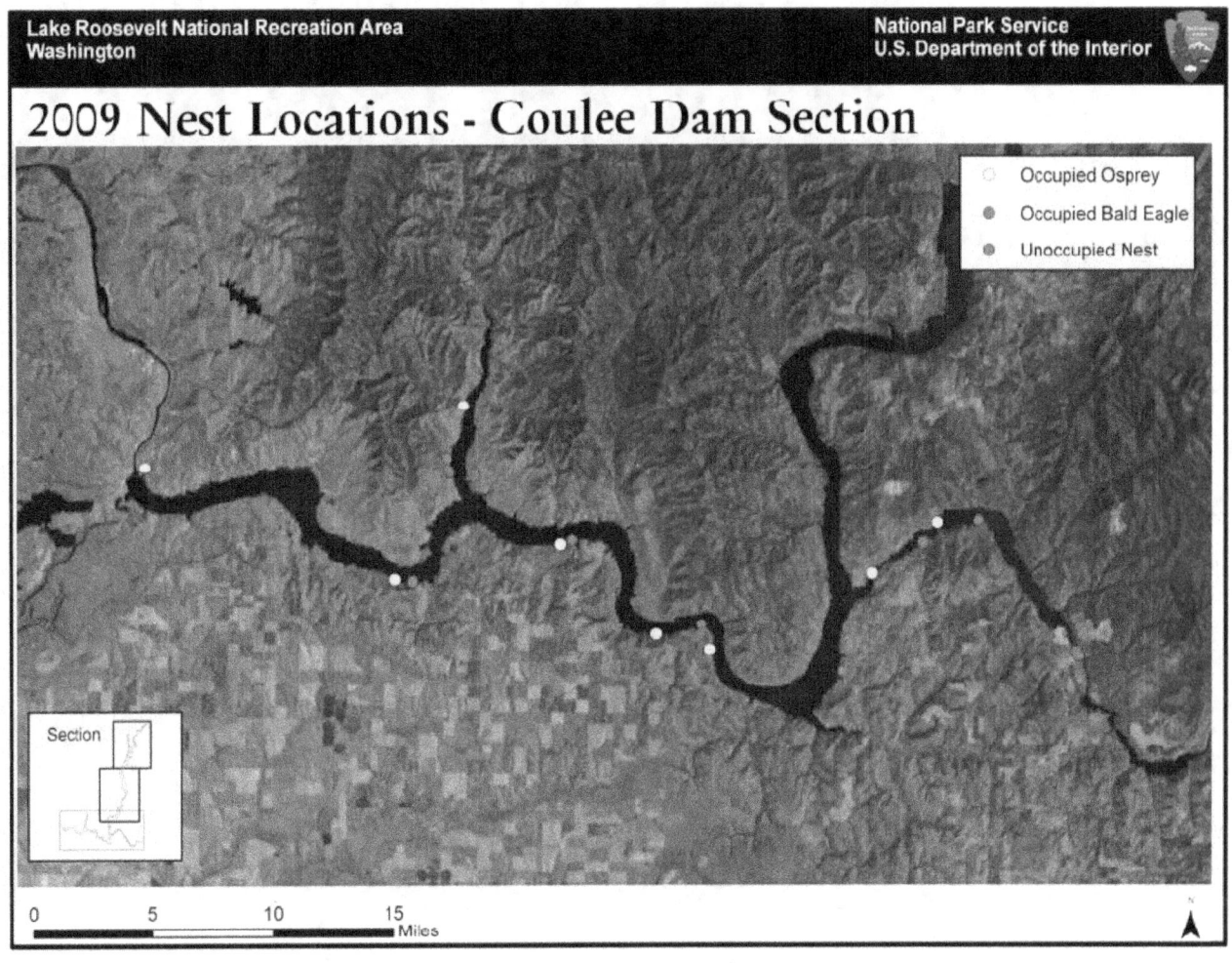

Appendix C. Map of nest site locations in LARO (2009 Gifford section)

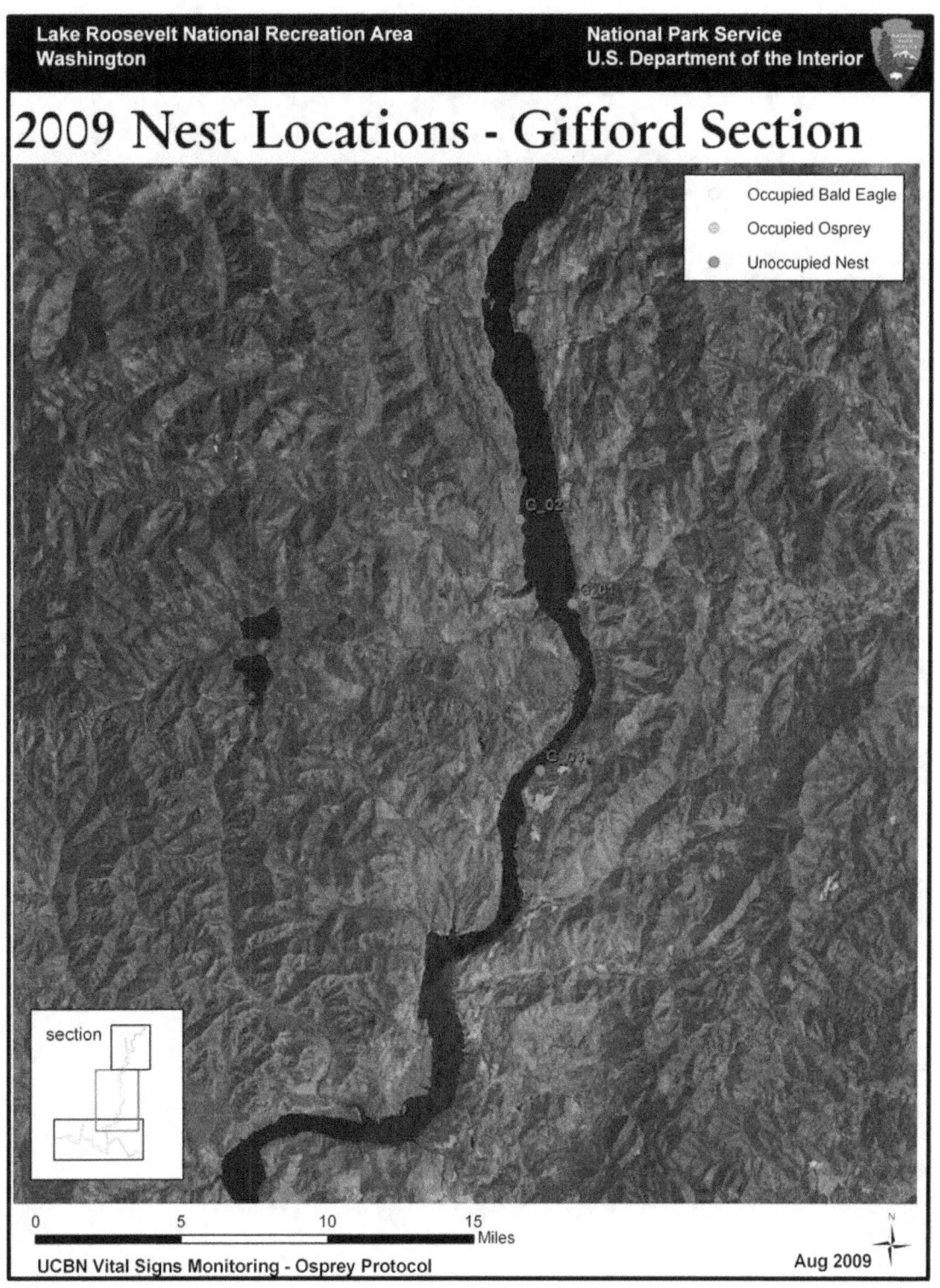

Appendix D. Map of nest site locations in LARO (2009 Kettle Falls section)

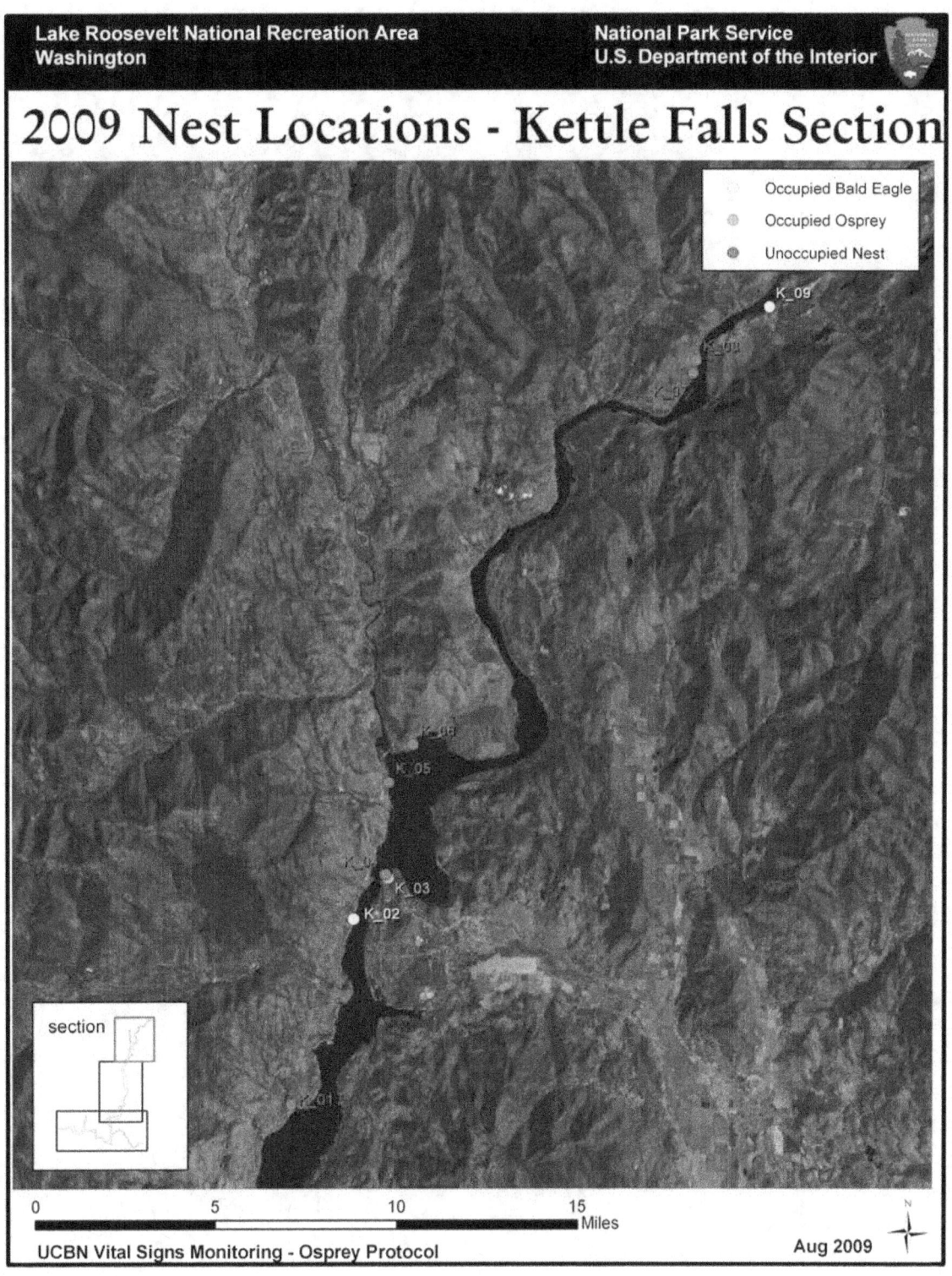

Appendix E. GPS coordinates of nest sites checked during the 2009 survey and occupancy status.

Nest ID	Species	Lake Section	UTM X (Easting)	UTM Y (Northing)	UTM Zone	Datum	Status 2009
C_03	Unknown	Coulee Dam	370700	5306446	11N	NAD83	Not occupied
C_04	Unknown	Coulee Dam	373199	5313519	11N	NAD83	Not occupied
C_05	Unknown	Coulee Dam	373112	5313761	11N	NAD83	Not occupied
C_07	Unknown	Coulee Dam	374356	5326513	11N	NAD83	Not occupied
C_09	Unknown	Coulee Dam	381434	5309149	11N	NAD83	Not occupied
C_14	Unknown	Coulee Dam	405205	5308979	11N	NAD83	Not occupied
C_16	Unknown	Coulee Dam	408981	5310390	11N	NAD83	Not occupied
C_17	Unknown	Coulee Dam	415548	5301773	11N	NAD83	Not occupied
C_18	Unknown	Coulee Dam	415688	5301520	11N	NAD83	Not occupied
C_19	Unknown	Coulee Dam	373026	5314534	11N	NAD83	Not occupied
G_01	Unknown	Gifford	414592	5350304	11N	NAD83	Not occupied
G_02	Unknown	Gifford	411688	5354819	11N	NAD83	Not occupied
G_03	Unknown	Gifford	412847	5341338	11N	NAD83	Not occupied
K_01	Unknown	Kettle Falls	413826	5376420	11N	NAD83	Not occupied
K_04	Unknown	Kettle Falls	418006	5386738	11N	NAD83	Not occupied
K_05	Unknown	Kettle Falls	418152	5390848	11N	NAD83	Not occupied
K_06	Unknown	Kettle Falls	419223	5392554	11N	NAD83	Not occupied
K_07	Unknown	Kettle Falls	431742	5409142	11N	NAD83	Not occupied
K_08	Unknown	Kettle Falls	431878	5409739	11N	NAD83	Not occupied
C_01	Osprey	Coulee Dam	352846	5313950	11N	NAD83	Occupied
C_02	Osprey	Coulee Dam	369515	5306571	11N	NAD83	Occupied
C_06	Osprey	Coulee Dam	374164	5317955	11N	NAD83	Occupied
C_08	Osprey	Coulee Dam	374164	5308886	11N	NAD83	Occupied
C_10	Osprey	Coulee Dam	387027	5302947	11N	NAD83	Occupied
C_12	Osprey	Coulee Dam	390643	5301951	11N	NAD83	Occupied
C_13	Osprey	Coulee Dam	401627	5306929	11N	NAD83	Occupied
C_15	Osprey	Coulee Dam	406169	5310267	11N	NAD83	Occupied
K_03	Osprey	Kettle Falls	418127	5386567	11N	NAD83	Occupied
C_11	Bald Eagle	Coulee Dam	390059	5303608	11N	NAD83	Occupied
K_02	Bald Eagle	Kettle Falls	416602	5384725	11N	NAD83	Occupied
K_09	Bald Eagle	Kettle Falls	435168	5412115	11N	NAD83	Occupied

NPS 963/106166, December 2010